Eradicating StupidITy: A Handbook for Smart IT Management

Harry Flowers

Second Edition

ISBN-13: 978-1530965403

ISBN-10: 1530965403

Dedication

I'd like to thank my wife, Karen, for editing the book and being so gracious about the time I spent writing it. Technology is not her thing, but she valiantly made it through and even liked it! I'd also like to thank Ricky Howell and Mike Old for their reviews and suggestions before publishing the first edition.

Contents

Preface

We've all heard it from others; we have thought it; we have shared it in confidence: **"What do they think they're doing?"** From those outside technology departments and those inside as well, it's often really hard to make sense of technology decisions. Sometimes it's because the decisions are bad ones, perhaps based on false assumptions. Sometimes the decisions are good, but communicating the reasons behind them and sharing the vision has been neglected. **This book is intended to both provide a framework to make good decisions as well as a methodology for sharing the vision and understanding behind them that is the key to cooperation across organizational boundaries.** At times, you may think I seem to be arguing with myself as I state the case both for and against various practices. That is intentional. This book is not about telling you what to do, but how to think about what to do. In the end, you have to decide what is best for your organization given all the technical factors, the political factors in your organization, and whatever market pressures influence your business.

Who should read this book? People who want to use technology to their advantage in their business. Board members, CEO's, business planners, and even information technology professionals may find this an interesting read. Most of this book is targeted to people working at medium to large enterprises, but small business leaders may also find much of it helpful.

I have a varied perspective that comes from being the only IT person to being one of thousands in a company. I've worked for and also contracted at Fortune 100 companies and ones with fewer than 100 employees. I've worked in the public and private sector, academia and business, and I have tried to use the wisdom gained from those perspectives in this book.

The first chapter is geared to senior level leadership, especially those who choose the senior IT leadership. The second chapter is directed toward senior IT leaders. Both chapters and subsequent chapters are for anyone with an interest in information technology.

Some of the edits for the second edition are shown as "2016 Update". I did this in cases where it was interesting to note the changes in two short years. Seeing what's changed and how much can be informative.

Warning!
Geek
Speak

In the course of this book, I'll put this warning before the more technical information. People who aren't interested in the more technical content can safely skip these sections or save them for late-night reading when you are having trouble getting to sleep. When the snooze section is over, you'll see this:

Returning You
to Non-Geek
Speak ☺

For the Kindle version, the smiley face symbol may be translated to a capital letter "J". So, if you see one of those hanging around by itself, it was meant to be a smiley face. Just pretend the "J" stands for jocularity. ☺

Chapter 1:
<u>Start at the Top</u>

The Chief Executive Officer (CEO) is ultimately responsible for everything in an organization. It follows, then, that if you as CEO aren't happy with your current technology or support, you are responsible for that, too. There are a few key areas that you can focus on.

Technology Is Critical to Success

If you are looking upon information technology (IT) as an expense, you are never going to be using it to your full advantage. The successful CEOs of today realize technology is a core part of almost every aspect of their business. If you need convincing, just look at the emergence and dominance of technology talks in investor meetings for publicly-held companies regardless of their industry. **IT used to be a back-office function that was not discussed in polite company; today it is recognized as strategic for continuing success.** Unfortunately, attitudes and beliefs often trail thought processes, and those who believed technology was a necessary evil are not quick to embrace all the ways it can be leveraged to transform your business.

Even if you plan on having people outside your business provide a significant portion of your IT services, someone in your organization needs to be asking the right questions to ensure the services fit your needs rather than just the bullet points in a brochure. **It's all too common for mistakes in the planning and selection stage to translate to failures in the implementation stage.** Most of the law suits brought by organizations over project failures by vendors have at their core a lack of understanding of what the true requirements were and exactly how the vendor's solution would meet them. Usually, the vendor is really selling a package that they think will meet most of the requirements and matching up their features with the closest thing on your requirements list. The organizations, on the other hand, are typically assuming that they are starting with their requirements and ensuring that everything is covered, even requirements that were implied but not stated.

With more and more services being offered needing little in the way of new technology resources within your business, it's tempting to let different groups within your organization purchase whatever products seem to be best. However, your IT organization is also a sanity check for vetting how well a particular product will work with others in your environment. If your marketing department wants to purchase this great customer relationship management (CRM) product as a cloud service that you later discover won't talk to your enterprise resource planning (ERP) system, your marketing and finance groups aren't going to be happy that their data's not updating between them. These things need to be worked out before you invest your money. Your organization may need to develop the interface between them and those costs need to be figured into the total costs for any implementation.

The IT industry of today is changing rapidly. If your IT operation is primarily going to be provided by your own staff, it's even more critical that they understand the changing landscape for datacenter management and software development environments. I'll cover disruptive technologies in a chapter towards the end of this book, but suffice it to say here that initiatives like "big data" require new software, tools, and infrastructure that are different in fundamental ways from what we're used to running. **Your technology leadership and staff are more important to the success of your business than ever before.** You need to be confident you are providing the technologies that best support your goals.

Choosing Leaders

I believe that **the most important leadership qualities for any position are these two "I"'s: integrity and imagination**. Without integrity, you can't trust what someone says or does in the present or future. Without imagination, a leader can't see things other than as a natural progression from the present. Since we're at a pivotal time with technologies that are truly disruptive (much more on that in the last chapter), the ability to envision a much different future from the *status quo* has benefits for every area of your organization. It is especially important for the top leaders, not just your technology officers.

Unfortunately, integrity and imagination are both difficult to determine at an interview. And, while references may be able to answer integrity questions if the answers are positive, how well someone used their imagination at past jobs would require a lot of thought for an answer.

I once wrote a white paper to help me show other leaders what I thought the technology future at our organization should look like and it was quite different from where we were and touched on how things would change for everyone. I also had the initial and recurring costs of maintaining that new normal, so I expect our chief financial officer (CFO) thought it quite practical in that sense. I don't know that they would have considered the imagination needed to see our organization doing business differently. It was a huge change for the employees, but one that was later often bragged about to other similar organizations who hadn't made similar provisions. Circling back to my point, imagination in someone else can be difficult to recognize, especially when it's wrapped up in business plans.

Traditionally, the Chief Information Officer (CIO) is the leader with specific responsibility for information technology (IT) within an organization. Sometimes they have a Chief Technology Officer (CTO) reporting to them. It's becoming increasingly more common to have a CTO as the leader and no CIO. I believe this trend can be attributed to a renewed focus on understanding technology for good decision-making and strategic planning. **This need for technical savvy is becoming increasingly more critical as the options for technology implementations have never been so broad.** I've also thought the Chief Information Officer title is somewhat misleading, since most information is controlled by the division that creates and utilizes it. Good auditing practices tend to enforce this idea. Information about personnel, for example, is typically controlled by a human resources department, legal counsel controls information about pending litigation, etc. Rather than the ultimate owner of all information, **IT plays a supporting role for information stewards in the entire organization** and is responsible for helping safeguard it whenever it is stored digitally.

I have been in several interviews for CIOs where the people being interviewed stated, "I'm not technical." What I assume they meant to imply by this (and what they expected their listeners to infer) are two things:

1. I can speak to other leaders in the business without using a lot of IT jargon that no one outside IT will understand.
2. I can keep focused on the overall picture for the business without getting mired in the technical details, leaving that to my staff.

What an organization really needs, though, is a technically-knowledgeable person who can do both of those things. That's because a technical knowledge and understanding can help keep the organization focused on goals that are advantageous and achievable. For every project idea that isn't feasible due to technical reasons, there are other project opportunities to improve business processes with technology that will.

Let's face it, you expect the chief officers to bring their areas of expertise to the table as well as a good understanding of how they relate to your business. The Chief Financial Officer (CFO) should bring expertise in finance, understanding things such as generally accepted accounting principles, present value of future income, and economics. He may not be the comptroller, budget director, or procurement specialist, but he should be able to understand everything they tell him and turn around and put it in layman's terms for others. Why would you settle for a CIO/CTO who can't bring the same level of expertise in technology to the table?

Now, by technical, I'm not talking about being able to list products and model numbers for a given task (that stuff changes all the time, anyway) or the commands or program lines to accomplish something. No, by technical, I'm talking about **understanding how the current state of the practice in information technology works with the ability to distinguish what's real, what's hype, and a good idea of what is coming down the road** to position your organization to be an early adopter of something that will really make a difference. They should have staff that will dig into the nitty-gritty of researching the best product fit for your needs and planning the acquisition and implementation. (I'll cover more about staffing and researching the best solutions later.) But, they should have no problem following and should already know most of the information like that in the "Geek Speak" section that follows.

So, you're not a techie geek... how can you tell if someone knows his bits from his bytes? My recommendation is to invite someone who is technologically knowledgeable along for at least one cycle of the interview process. Perhaps you know a CTO working elsewhere that might give you their feedback? Or, perhaps you trust the opinion of someone in your IT department that doesn't want the top slot but would be happy to help vet someone else for the position? You know the business aptitude you're looking for and they can help ensure you also hire someone with the technical aptitude needed to really give your business the tech boost it needs! The next time you hear "I'm not technical" in a job interview for your IT leadership, you should let the candidate know how disappointed you are to hear that and see how they follow it up. [1] ☺

For example, in the rise of cloud computing we're seeing today, it is a great advantage to have IT leadership who understand the concepts of "latency" and "bandwidth". Simply put, latency is the delay from when you send a request to when you receive the response. Bandwidth refers to the maximum rate (usually in some power of bits per second) at which requests and responses can be transmitted.

Simple latency example: You're talking on the phone. You ask a question and then wait for a response. The latency is the time from when you stop speaking and start waiting for the reply until you hear the reply begin. You expect the response on the phone to be within a few seconds. If not, you're going to follow-up with a query to see if the person heard you. The length of time you wait before repeating or following up on your question is called your "timeout". If you're expecting phone conversation latency and get text message latency (where you're expecting to wait minutes or hours), you're going to give up and hang up the phone. This also works in the computer world. Applications that are expecting a reasonable response for the type of communication they are doing will timeout waiting for a reply and do the equivalent of hanging up.

Simple bandwidth example: You're pouring a liquid from one bottle into another using a funnel. The smallest part of the funnel restricts how much liquid will flow through. If you're pouring from the other bottle and the stream of liquid never exceeds the size of the funnel, you're staying within the bandwidth of that funnel. If you pour faster, then the liquid will start gathering up the sides of the funnel. In computer terms, we'd say the funnel is caching the liquid until it can be transmitted into the bottle below.

If you don't stop or slow down your pouring, you'll overflow the funnel.

It's easy for people to think bandwidth equals speed. Even the companies that sell it call it "high-speed Internet". However, **electronic data travels over the wires at the speed of the electrons (near the speed of light); for a given medium it's a constant**. Data actually travels at the same speed regardless of your bandwidth until you reach the limit of your bandwidth, when it has to be cached and paused. It's better to think of it as the rate of flow in our funnel example above. More bandwidth is using a funnel with a bigger opening. If you're trickling data down it, it doesn't matter how big the funnel is. If you want to stream video down it, you need a bigger funnel than if you're just grabbing text files from a web server.

From these examples, we can also deduce that **bandwidth only effects latency when you're trying to exceed the rated limit**. The caching of the data that exceeds the bandwidth adds a delay to when it reaches the other side of the funnel, which adds to the latency. Internet service providers who have allowed their bandwidth to frequently be saturated (usually at peering points with other providers) are becoming an increasingly significant problem for both bandwidth and latency as Internet usage continues to expand.

So, why is all this important for understanding cloud computing? It's because distance is a big factor in increased latency. Since we haven't figured out how to break the laws of physics to go faster than the speed of light (or warp space for our data connections, if you prefer your science fiction that way), it's impossible to get the same latency from a remote location as a local one. Here are the two main contributors to distance latency that no amount of additional bandwidth can address:

1. Each switch or router in the path adds latency. Typically, routers will buffer the packet until it receives the end. Then, it spends time evaluating where to send the packet

based on the rules loaded into it. Routers that do "deep packet inspection" don't just look at the headers, but also the data portion of the packet to determine things like the quality of service the packet should receive.

2. The maximum speed for the data is the speed of light (whether you're sending electrons across a wire, photons across fiber optical cables, or transmitting it wirelessly via radio waves). The latency is double the distance since you are sending and waiting for the reply (the data has to get there and you are waiting to get the response back even if it's just the acknowledgment it was received). If you don't think this is important, consider that a lot of effort is spent laying cable across ocean floors rather than going the longer distance up to a satellite and back.

For example, you can't place the disk storage that a server is expecting to be local at a remote location because the device drivers on the server will assume the disks are not working when they don't respond quickly enough. In addition, even if you could increase the timeout values, you would slow a server down incredibly by only having such storage available since every disk access would be orders of magnitude slower.

On the other hand, some applications, like web servers, are designed for high latency between the web browser and the server. You won't see a huge performance degradation going from a local server to one in the cloud.

Some applications fall in between in terms of latency requirements. It's not generally recommended to place an application server and the database server it is constantly hitting at different sites. It might work, but the performance will be disappointing even if it does.

Understanding these concepts and what types of applications are tolerant of high latency can save your business a lot of time and money when you're considering cloud computing options. Trying to split resources that have low latency requirements to one or more geographically diverse cloud providers will fail. Understanding that and redesigning how you go about achieving your goal (perhaps by replicating data so it's "local" at each site) may still allow what you are trying to accomplish overall.

Returning You
to Non-Geek
Speak ☺

Casting Vision

Everyone from the board room to the mail room should know your business goals. Sure, you may not have a board room or mail room, but you understand what I'm saying. If you want people to pull together, they need a clear idea of what the goals are to know what direction to pull. Otherwise, they're going to pull in whatever direction seems best for them, which won't generally leave everyone pulling the same way.

Ideas may come from the bottom, but vision has to be cast from the top of your organization. If you have a strategic plan for your business with clear, attainable goals, your business units can develop their own goals and objectives in support of them. In today's environment, business units should work together on their goals as the interdependence between units has never been greater. The goals a traditional business unit has have to be tempered with what resources other units have to support them and need to be supported by them. Planning in silos assuming everything the other units are doing will have similar impact as they did last year is more problematic than ever before. Several disruptive technologies are reshaping the business landscape and they've only just begun.

What's that have to do with the overall vision? It should include increased collaboration. I don't mean spending a lot of money on collaboration tools, though that could be a part of what might need to happen. No, at the vision level, you set the expectation that the traditional divisional boundaries are primarily useful for the division of labor, but everyone is expected to understand and be familiar with the goals not only of the business as a whole, but of every other division and what their own part might be in making them successful, and in turn, adding those objectives to their own business unit after consulting with the goal unit on how they could best be aided. Leaders in every part of your organization need to be "big picture" people that see how their work interrelates to the whole.

Your IT leadership needs to be able to cast a technology vision from your business vision and follow that up with goals and measurable objectives that will support the goals and objectives of other business units.

PLAN Is More Than a Four-letter Word

Strategic planning seems to have fallen out of vogue. Project planning, on the other hand, is big right now. Most large businesses have already set up project management offices (PMO) to oversee project planning. While executing projects well is important, it's even more important choosing which projects to implement and sharing a clear understanding of where they fall within supporting your overall strategy. I'm not going to spend time on this very important point because there are many excellent management books[2] that already cover this topic better than I could. If you're in management, you've probably already read many of them. So, I'm only going to cover some of the practical outcomes of planning.

The following conversation between Alice and the Cheshire Cat from Lewis Carroll's *Alice's Adventures in Wonderland* illustrates the point well:

> Alice said, "`Would you tell me, please, which way I ought to go from here?'
> `That depends a good deal on where you want to get to,' said the Cat.
> `I don't much care where –,' said Alice.

18

`Then it doesn't matter which way you go,' said the Cat.
`– so long as I get *somewhere*,' Alice added as an explanation."

Without a vision of where you want to go, it doesn't matter what projects you do because you'll always end up someplace. However, if desire to get to someplace in particular, then you need a vision of where you want to wind up, goals to aim for that will establish that, and objectives that should be met to accomplish those goals. **You can have the most efficient project management process in existence that is still not effective because you're not initiating the best projects to improve your business.**

There are two major knowledge areas required to make good technology plans:

1. Know your vertical market. If the market is growing rapidly and you're positioned well, you might have a goal to maintain your market share and grow your business. If the market is mature or declining, you're probably looking to increase your market share and/or diversify into an area that is growing. Successful companies do this very well; it is the key to their success.

2. Know the technology market. Keeping up with emerging technologies and their strengths and weaknesses will help position your business to take advantage of them at the right time or, just as importantly, pass on ones that aren't right for you at the time. I'll cover this in detail in chapter three.

Goals and objectives with any technology components should be set on the basis of both areas of knowledge. The **objectives should be specific and measurable**. If you use vague words such as "better" or "improve" in your goals, that's okay though not ideal. But, the objectives should spell out exactly how you're going to measure a specific aspect of that improvement, what specific benchmarks you are aiming for, and over what period of time. A single goal may have many objectives that lead to fulfilling it. You should have no doubts whether you've met your objectives or not. For example, a goal could be "improve IT helpdesk support". That's quite vague. However, the objectives associated with it could be "reduce average phone on hold time from twenty seconds to ten seconds", "reduce time tickets are in helpdesk queue unassigned to a maximum of four hours", "close tickets not waiting on client response within forty-eight hours", etc. These specific and measurable objectives show what you mean by "improve IT helpdesk support".

I remember sitting in one of those day-long meetings at a leadership retreat about mission, vision, and goals. The president had as part of his new vision statement becoming the leading organization in our region for our market. I thought, "That's great! I can't wait to hear what goals he has in mind to lead us toward that!" I was very disappointed when he had none. He evidently didn't know what that would look like to share it with us. It was merely a wish he had, not something he expected to accomplish.

At another organization, we spent a lot of time talking about planning. We had lots of "planning to plan" meetings in our division. But, for all that, very little actual planning went on. Leaders didn't have clear objectives because there weren't clear goals and objectives for the business outside our division, and without those to set a direction, all they could do was talk about planning. They knew they needed to plan better, but they didn't have the necessary information to be effective planners. **Incoming projects appeared like blips on the radar** and, like air traffic controllers, we just tried to make sure they had a safe landing. It would have been lovely to have helped develop their flight plans beforehand so we could provide direction and navigational aids to make both flights and landings less bumpy.

If planning isn't being coordinated at the top, the best the underlying business units can do is plan to maintain the

status quo, **assume linear growth in resource needs, and make plans that are flexible enough to accommodate minor changes to that.** If you want to allow for major improvements to your business, that won't do.

Communicate!

This is usually on everyone's short list of things to improve in any organization, so why does it stay there? We have to be very intentional about communication. It has to start at the top, both talking and listening. Support for communication at every level and business unit is critical.

I was the IT leader at one organization when I was informed it was very likely we would merge with a sister organization. Armed with this knowledge, I began changing my criteria for procurement to include how well it might work with them. We were planning on replacing our phone switch at our main business campus. Our sister organization had just been through that. Instead of looking just for what might best fit our campus, I considered how well our new switch would integrate with theirs and how well it would work if the merger didn't go through. We ended up purchasing the same model switch since it would have done a good job for us alone but had many added benefits if we merged. The merger went through, and we were able to connect the switches to allow extension-only dialing from either site. This not only smoothed the process of the IT part of the merger, but aided communications overall and gave a sense that we were a single organization much more quickly and directly. This was especially important because the merger was not universally warmly received and anything we could do to put everyone on the same footing was very helpful to overall morale. Without communication from the CEO of the likely merger, we would have faced a more costly and difficult integration.

How can you tell if you're communicating enough? One indicator is the business rumor mill. Lack of communication is grist for the mill; the more rumors there are, the more need there is to communicate. Replace rumors with clear messages and the workplace will be much healthier. Correct information consistently shared tends to kill rumors and unify business units. If you have no information to share where rumors are starting, that's an indicator that maybe there needs to be more planning in that area so that there is something to communicate. The presence of the rumor beyond the usual gossips often indicates there was an unmet need for information.

Whether you use e-mails, wikis, meetings, conference calls, or even written memos, you should set an expectation that information must be readily available. The more everyone knows about what is going on and feels that their contributions have been heard, the more sense of personal ownership and responsibility they will feel toward meeting the objectives for their units and the more sense of accomplishment they will feel when those objectives are met or surpassed.

On the upward information flow side, the more constructive feedback to goals and objectives management has, the more they can improve the objectives and gain ideas for new goals.

So far, we've been discussing communication in general. That does need to be addressed first. But, there are specific needs regarding technology as well.

It's never been a particularly good idea to have your IT staff too sequestered from the rest of your business. In order to combat this, some businesses have gone so far as to embed their IT folks within other business units. For most businesses, the ideal lies somewhere in between. It really boils down to facilitating good communications. There are two competing objectives:

1. IT folks need to be in a position to hear and respond to the business needs of the entire organization. **It's much better to work from the goal than some proposed solution where the original goal is obscured. You might execute the solution perfectly and still not**

meet the need. Throwing proposed solutions "over the wall" to IT to implement is a common mistake.

2. IT folks need to be in a position to gain from each other's experiences so that they don't keep redeveloping the same types of solutions starting from scratch, in essence wasting resources to "reinvent the wheel". They also need to adhere to the same standards as much as possible (more on the increasing importance of standards later).

In practice, organizationally IT works best as a centralized group with a lot of cross-representation among the units it supports. For example, an IT representative in the applications support department could attend business meetings dealing with enterprise resource planning (ERP), while a representative from that business unit could attend IT meetings in which ERP software was the focus. It would be mutually beneficial. "IT governance" was a popular term for organizing committees that ensure all business units have representation in technology planning. The current trend in the meaning of "IT governance" now primarily involves project oversight, security, and compliance within the IT organization and the emphasis on business unit coordination has largely been lost.

While it's important to keep open lines between IT departments and the rest of business, it's equally important to do the same within IT. The "DevOps" movement grew out of a need for developers and operations within IT to work more closely together to improve agile development support while improving infrastructure stability and flexibility at the same time; these goals will be at odds with each other without careful coordination between groups and shared responsibility for the final products. I'll be covering agile development methodology in more detail later.

I've noticed a trend for DevOps that it has mainly come to mean adopting cloud architecture tools for provisioning servers. Rather than changing software installed on existing servers, the goal is the ability to deploy a replacement as many times a day as you'd like with the new software installed. This means that in addition to automatic provisioning of the servers and operating systems, all post-installation configuration has to be scripted so little or no manual intervention is required. The more complex the environment, the more difficult it is to achieve. Also, while that's good for development and test servers, there hasn't been a change management model that supports doing that in production where you want only reliable fully-tested servers deployed. Rapid deployment and change management methodologies have conflicting requirements; only time will tell how the DevOps movement will manage to accommodate both and with what compromises.

Any changes in IT with client-side implications should have representatives of those clients involved. Procurement that would result in changes in e-mail, collaboration software, phones, or office software suites should all have extensive representation from the user community. **Always look at who will be directly impacted.** If you have a storage management group that is investigating new storage area network (SAN) controllers and storage, their main clients are the systems engineers who will be using the presented storage. They should have representation in the selection process. End users want their services to work so they expect you to choose something stable that performs well, but unless your company is in the IT business, they're not going to be interested in the details. Infrastructure is much the same everywhere; when I flip a light switch, I want power to the bulb, but I don't care which type of generators are used in the power plant. On the other hand, if you want to switch out light fixtures, I might have some interest if it includes the one over my desk. Identify your client audience and proceed accordingly.

However your business is organized, **never let organizational structure dictate process. Your organizational structure is there to support what needs doing, not the other way**

around. If your organizational structure is an impediment to progress, change it. The process of changing it may also help solidify in everyone's mind what you're trying to accomplish. Just make sure you have clear goals for the change so everyone understands and you can evaluate afterwards how successful the changes were in accomplishing the goals.

IT Flows Downhill

The tone you set at the top determines a lot about how your IT units will operate. If new ideas are discouraged, then they will rarely be given. Projects will be on the conservative side and "done how we've always done" them. On the other hand, if you start projects while you're still brainstorming ideas, you'll tend to have a lot of failures. You need to communicate how conservative you want to be. I think encouraging some risk-taking and pilot projects where you're okay with using it as a learning experience with a less-than-ideal outcome is positive overall. The more critical projects need to be carefully planned and executed. Don't let a pilot project turn into a critical one mid-project (unless you can leverage early success and plan the remainder more carefully).

The majority of people don't like change, though some thrive on it. In IT, change is the only constant. The tone for how change is managed is also set at the top. Don't sell your folks short thinking they won't embrace changes with clear benefits. If they've been in an IT career very long, they've already experienced many changes in how they work. On the other hand, if they're new in the field, they aren't used to a particular way of doing things. Either way, IT folks are likely to be among the most receptive to change in your organization.

Speaking of change, I've seen many sales people try the "resistant to change" line on IT leadership to get them on board with their product or service when they know it's met resistance for technical reasons down the line. Sadly, they've been successful at it some of the time. If you have technical expertise on your staff, their talks with the sales engineers are worth far more than whatever hype cycle sales representatives or magazines are touting at the time. I'm not trying to denigrate sales representatives here: their job is to sell you goods and services, and a good sales representative will try whatever seems to work well in your environment. If getting the CIO to make unilateral decisions works, that's an indictment on the leadership, not the sales representatives.

Security

Why am I putting IT security in this chapter? Technology has never been more pervasive in our society and our businesses and that trend just keeps accelerating. We can't relegate security concerns to our IT folks; it's **everyone's responsibility**. A recent loss of payment card industry (PCI) data by a large retail franchise resulted in requests for personnel changes for the CEO *and* board members by shareholders. Never has there been more need for non-geeks to be involved in securing their technology, not just at work, but personal devices at home. As even light bulbs start coming with wireless networking, the level of technology security consciousness must rise in the general population.

IT security is basically the practice of making it more difficult for non-authorized persons to access programs, information, or devices that they have no legitimate reason to access. There is no perfectly secure system that is still usable (the old joke about encasing a system in concrete and burying it deep still is not perfect☺). It's all a matter of how difficult you are willing to make accessing your systems with the trade-off of ease of use and how much you can afford to spend securing them. Here are some guidelines:

1. **IT security is everyone's business.** It's just as important for staff outside IT to be knowledgeable about IT security and feel that they are a part of protecting information. Most spear phishing[3] hackers are targeting folks outside IT security areas. Some people want to foist it off on IT ("let them worry about that"), but they are a part of your protection. Those same people would be

complaining if IT locked everything down to the point where it would be very difficult for them to compromise security. If your corporate culture is one in which people don't feel they should be bothered about security, that needs to change and soon!

2. **Don't worry about government spy agencies.** Yes, you read that right. If they want your data, they will get it. Unless you're in the business of dealing with top secret information, it's definitely not going to be worth the expense to put something in place that would actually thwart them.[4] If you happen to be a company that deals with top secret security, the measures you need to take are far beyond the scope of this book. For the vast majority of organizations, **your focus should be on securing your IT resources from hackers and others that have an interest in your resources or data.** That is the real and persistent threat that influences the level of security you need to implement and justifies the costs of your security implementation.

3. **Do worry about third-party vendors you use.** The majority of companies that I've seen install software on sites where I've worked left things a mess security-wise. This includes companies with "security" in their name. Installers sometimes take shortcuts getting things to work and don't come back to tighten down security afterwards. Many companies don't actually have folks in their product line units that understand IT security very well. Some of the highly publicized data breaches happened through their vendors.

4. People don't want to invest time and effort on security until there's been a breach, but good **security procedures are designed to prevent breaches before they occur**, not when it's too late. A healthy degree of paranoia is good for IT folks, especially in the infrastructure areas of networks, servers, and storage. If you have a separate Information Security department, they should work closely together on provisioning procedures. After all, **there *are***

people after your IT resources and data. There are lots of best practices for encryption, networking, and securing servers and storage. Take whatever reasonable steps you have available to increase security. The more sensitive the information, the more effort it is worth to secure.

Chapter 2:
<u>Below "C" Level</u>

So, you've got your chief-level officer with some chief officer title that is technically knowledgeable. Unless you were able to promote from within, their first months on the job will be learning about your market and organizational culture. They will be assessing your IT capabilities, strengths, and weaknesses. They will also be developing impressions of the skill level of their staff. This chapter is all about the managers and staff within the IT division.

If you look at a spreadsheet listing all the current IT assets, the biggest asset will be missing: people. These are the people that make technology work at your business. These people enable others to do their jobs as well. For all my emphasis on technology, it all falls flat without the people to make it happen.

I'm going somewhat against the tide here when I say that people really are your most valuable assets. Oh, lots of companies will say this, but actions always speak louder than words. Most of the current thinking is that you can contract out anything you want to do and end up paying less than you would with your own employees. While none of us are irreplaceable, **people bring a unique combination of expertise and experience to their roles and retain valuable knowledge of past projects in your organization as well as acclamation to your corporate culture**. While it's also advantageous to get a fresh perspective from new hires, an annual turnover rate of greater than twenty percent means a lot of specific business knowledge is going out the door. It also means a lot of your staff are new and working on getting "up to speed" on your projects, tools, and environment. Your more experienced staff are the ones spending time on helping them, so neither group is as productive. Next time you're considering replacing an employee with a contractor, remember to factor in something for the cost of turnover and the opportunity costs of what could have been accomplished by someone already in place.

Contracting and Outsourcing

You may think I'm anti-outsourcing from the paragraph above. I'm not and I've been on both sides of this. But, I think the best value for a company in hiring contractors is when it's for a "one-off" type project. If you're going to be doing whatever it is long term, you're much better off with your own employees for a number of reasons, some of which I stated above. Contracting and outsourcing pretty much guarantees increased turnover.

If you lack the expertise you need among your staff, contracting is an attractive option. **If you have a small business and only occasionally need the help, finding a good partner consulting business is a great option.** If you are larger and are going to need the expertise full time, you might consider "contract to hire" positions to get these people on staff.

Morale is another consideration when outsourcing. If you've got employees and contractors doing the same jobs, it can cause tension. The employees may be envious of the amount you're paying for the contractor (not that the contractor is seeing as much of that as they might think) and the contractors may be envious of the perceived job stability and benefits of the employees. Add in that there are invariably some employees and some contractors that are better suited to the jobs than others and you have a recipe for some grumbling on both sides.

If a core part of your IT is involved, why contract it out? A contracting company has to make money for the account representatives and recruiters and their office space and compensation on top of the salary and benefits it pays to its employees who do the work for you. On top of that, you have contract negotiations, statements of work (SOW), and service level agreements (SLA) to iron out that require resources from both you and the contractor. **If all other things remained equal, they could not provide employees as cost effectively as you can by direct hiring.** You also don't get to select who you think is the best fit for the job (without the danger of appearing to be the employer and risk having to pay benefits anyway after a law suit). **However, all other things do not remain equal.** Typically, you pay more up front per hour than you pay your own employees. Ostensibly this is less than the total compensation package you'd pay an employee. I have my doubts about some cost calculations since the incremental cost per employee is often not used in favor of the total cost per employee; unless you're getting rid of all employees, a portion of that cost isn't flexible. The other side of this is they usually provide fewer benefits to their employees who are doing the contract work. If the employees are working remotely from another country, the total compensation can also be a fraction of what it is in your country. **You should also be aware of the communications challenges introduced by language and time zone differences; even global companies with employees already in these countries may be surprised by the challenges of coordinating contractors globally on projects.** The contracting company usually comes out ahead, your organization may or may not, and the people doing the work may be at a disadvantage.

There may be benefits in contracting for organizations in countries or states that do not have "work at will" laws that may tie an employer to an employee beyond their usefulness. There are also often internal political reasons chosen for going with contractors that have nothing to do with their suitability. I am not so naïve as to not realize that the political often overrules the practical. For example, if you're trying to make your organization look "lean and mean", you can give the impression of doing more with fewer human resources when your actual human resources aren't all employees (although I don't recommend this particular practice). Or, if the political environment is such that more employees are out of the question but contractors are okay, you do the best you can with the constraints you have (and try to remove constraints that aren't in the organization's best interests along the way).

Since I published the first edition of this book, I've seen more cases of outsourcing pains at fairly large companies. This becomes all too evident when leaving one vendor and either bring the work back in-house or going to another vendor. There's a severe lack of knowledge transfer and meta-data loss (information about exactly what work each application or server is performing, where your data all resides and all the backups or snapshots, etc.) One organization with which I'm familiar is in year three of getting things back together after one vendor's mess, and it'll probably take them another couple of years to fully recover. It's definitely something to factor into your decisions.

In summary, small businesses can benefit the most from contracting and outsourcing where they have occasional or part-time needs for expertise they do not have on staff. Larger organizations should look at the actual incremental cost for hiring an employee or group of employees versus a contractor or group of contractors rather than some "total cost per employee" figure determined by including overhead that would not change. Factor in turnover and missed opportunity costs for each scenario. Sometimes contracting makes sense, sometimes it doesn't. Just make sure you are using good information for the decisions and you should be happy with the outcomes.

Management: It's About Leadership

Many of the same principles apply to hiring managers as the chief technology officer. They should be expected to have more expertise in their area of supervision as well as have good leadership skills. Here are the qualities that make a good leader:

1. Ability to share vision, goals, and priorities with their unit and welcome feedback
2. Promptly deal with issues brought to their attention that affect staff or project completion; clearing away obstacles

that are holding up progress is one of the major roles of a manager

3. Ability to organize teams with staff whose individual strengths are needed for success
4. Expertise to maintain reasonable expectations and workloads for their staff
5. Ability to communicate effectively with other managers both inside and outside of IT up or down the management chain of command

It is sad to run across the "my way or the highway" type manager. They typically expect everyone to have the same strengths and also expect all their staff to adapt to dealing with them in a fixed manner instead of tailoring the interaction to what works best to motivate that individual. Markus Buckingham has made a successful career out of the message that people should take advantage of their strengths and improving them rather than focusing on weaknesses that, at best, might be brought up to average.

Another problem that often arises is the idea of what skills a manager needs. There is a misconception that seems to be propagated by organizations selling management courses that a manager can manage anyone, regardless of occupation. In reality, **shared expertise in the areas he or she manages is critical to being a good manager and necessary to mentoring or coaching those that may need it as well as accurate evaluation of resources required to perform given tasks**.

A good leader is one that enables people to do the best job they can with the resources they are provided. A manager needs enough knowledge of the skill areas reporting to them to be able to judge resources. One place I worked, my boss wanted me to fire one of my managers. I'd only been on the job there a few weeks myself, but I'd been keeping an eye on his area as a troubled one and determined that he was understaffed to do the job we were asking of him. He had a difficult job with a lot of project management involved and coordinating work for his staff. I convinced my boss to give him the personnel resources he needed (two people in this case) and then we could re-evaluate his job performance. We did that, and he did well. It was still up to him to come through on the job; I just made it doable.

Speaking of doable jobs, I sometimes have to chuckle at the range of expertise I see in job requirements, typically from small companies. I've been in jobs where I was the entire IT department, and I know the challenges of being a "one man army". You have to know a little about a lot of things and a lot about a few things – "a jack of all trades and master of some". If they really need masters of all those disciplines within IT, they would be a good candidate for contracting with a consulting company where they can get parts of different people's time and expertise as needed.

The Rise of the Architects

Back in the "old days" of IT, there was a little time built into people's jobs for research and development in their areas of expertise; time not spent on projects or closing work requests. In the push to "do more with less", most of that time has been taken away. After all, you can only do less with less unless you change what you are doing in some fundamental way that saves you time. Even though increased automation has brought on some of these fundamental changes, the continued push for "do more with less" has still eaten away at research time because the "more" has been growing exponentially and outpacing the automation time savings. Because technology never stops changing, this created a knowledge gap in the ability to implement new technologies. After all, if everyone is manning a bucket to bail water needed to keep a boat from sinking, no one can be spared to learn how to operate that newfangled pump contraption. ☺

IT architect jobs began to be created in order to ensure someone was able to investigate new technologies and design their introduction and use into the environment. There are infrastructure architects (who deal in networks, servers, storage, and the virtualization of those), information architects (who deal in database technologies and analytics, including the expanding "big data" pushes), and application architects (who deal in software design, application development, tools, and environments). Although the title "enterprise architect" is popular now, it could mean any of these types; judging from job descriptions, it usually refers to application architects with information architects a close second and infrastructure architects a distant third. These people are responsible for researching best fits for technology needs and developing reference architectures for their repeated implementation.

Good reference architectures are important for two reasons:

1. Since the implementations will be carried out by others, it's important to have the intended usage well documented so it can be implemented the same way any number of times.
2. Increased automation is dependent on increased standardization. If reference architectures are too vague, they do not make good standards documents. Failure to implement an architecture in a standard way will result in the inability to automate around it.

I admit to having mixed feelings about the rise of architects (even though I have had that role myself). I don't think it's necessarily good to get too separated from the folks that manage the equipment or software. A perfectly good product architecture can have failings because the vendor's support is lacking, and an architect won't know that without keeping in close touch with the people on the operations side. On the other hand, not all the operational folks are that interested in researching architecture, so keeping the research embedded in operations is also not a perfect solution. It's just another case of needing to keep the lines of communication open, in this case between architects and engineers.

Standardization and Automation

I already started on this in the architect section, but it deserves more discussion. The biggest productivity gains you can make will come from standardization. Here's why:

1. The more alike things are, the fewer resources it takes to support multiple instances of them.
2. Opportunities for automation arise from standardization. You can't automate when everything is different.

Of course, standardization doesn't work if everything has an exception to the standard. Likewise, people who say "We believe in standards... we have hundreds of them" have missed the boat. How many standard architectures you have largely depends on what types of things you're doing, but keep it to a minimum.

When an exception really is required, you have to be flexible enough to support it. The exception process should be:

1. Difficult enough where it's easier to change how something is done when possible.
2. Straight forward enough that people don't find ways around the process altogether.

Oftentimes folks who say they don't have time to do something right end up miraculously having even more time to do it over when they discover it doesn't work.

Agile Software Development Lifecycle

I've seen a lot of implementations of agile software development over the last five years. Odds are that your company is using or investigating agile development if you or your contractors do any computer software development. While it's not new, there are still many misconceptions about it. **Business analysts that are great at taking client input and turning that into program and data designs are worth their weight in gold no matter what methodology you use.**

Twentieth Century Software Development

Here's the brief history. Programming used to use a fairly structured sequential phase methodology: analyze, design, program, implement, and maintain. One phase is completed before the next; this is now commonly known as the waterfall method, though perhaps cascade would have been a better term to illustrate that one step happens after the other. It was great for planning and predictable outcomes giving the client exactly what they asked for. Unfortunately, **what a client asks for when they haven't seen anything of the application yet and what they need can sometimes be quite different things**. After the analysis phase, the client wasn't involved again until beta testing before the implementation phase. All the designing and programming is essentially complete except for addressing defects by then, and it's too late to have much impact on the final product.

Agile: Another Option for the Twenty-first Century

In 2001, the "Agile Manifesto" was written. The agile software development lifecycle is designed to present pieces of software as they're developed to get client feedback as to how it meets their needs. The agility to change the targeted designs as you go is what makes Agile. So, they might get to interact with the web interface before it does much of anything with the data, but can give feedback about how the interface fits their needs before a lot of the logic in handling the data is in place. As more functionality is added, its usefulness and fit to the needs of the clients are evaluated. Changes can be made in the design before the programming has progressed so far that it isn't feasible. **You should end up with a product more closely aligned with your client needs** than was possible under the waterfall methodology.

One of the most popular methods of implementing the Agile iterative environment is known as "Scrum". The iterative cycles in this case are called "sprints", and are typically two weeks long. Planning for the next sprint and demoing the current state of the software for the clients happens at the end of each one. As a sports analogy, sprint falls short because it implies going all out and completing the race; perhaps "laps" in the race would have been better, since most development projects more closely resemble marathons than sprints. You can't win a marathon without planning your pace for the long haul.

There is a daily scrum meeting that is fifteen minutes long and all the attendees remain standing if they are able. It's too bad that American football wasn't used instead of rugby for the metaphor, because the "huddle" there is more descriptive of what happens in a daily scrum: it's about sharing information with the team, not two teams vying for control (if you do have two teams vying for control in your daily scrums, you've got some team dynamic problems to address). Each team member shares what they did yesterday, what they plan to do today, and identifies any potential obstacles they might anticipate to achieving the sprint goals.

Another difference between waterfall and Agile is the software implementation schedule. On Agile projects, software often goes into production while still being actively developed once it's "far enough" along in functionality. This can lead to using some work-arounds for things like searches and reports that are still being developed, e.g., by direct database searches and reporting. This tends to get it in the hands of more client users and an increase in defect reporting and enhancement requests is typical at this point.

Common Pitfalls to Avoid with Agile Development
The strength of Agile is the feedback loop with the client.
If your client isn't giving feedback at the end of each sprint, you're missing the primary advantage of the Agile methodology. Here are some important points to keep in mind:

1. **Defining project scope is critical to project success for any development project.** Scope creep is the number one cause of project failure. **It's even more important to define the scope of your project for Agile methods because the iterative nature of the development almost encourages changing the**

scope of what you set out to accomplish. If you are changing scope, that needs to be clearly acknowledged by all stakeholders and clearly communicated up the management structure rather than letting the project scope just keep growing and wondering why you're never any closer to project completion.

2. **Agile requires more planning than waterfall.** Because the analysis and design done at the beginning is minimal compared to waterfall, some people believe that less time is spent planning. But, Agile requires that planning happens in every sprint. Because it's spread out over the entire development cycle and Agile is more change-friendly, more planning is done and possibly redone as the project progresses.

3. **Agile is not a substitute for planning.** This is almost a corollary to the previous point. Some folks mistakenly use partial Agile methods just to avoid having to do the analysis required for waterfall projects but don't involve the clients until it's almost complete as if it were a waterfall project. **This results in something worse than if either methodology were used correctly; you have insufficient feedback through the process and you haven't gathered enough requirements to be successful.**

4. **Management expectations for Agile projects must fit the framework.** Target dates for agile projects may change with each sprint. While that's part of the beauty of the flexibility of Agile projects, traditional deadline-oriented managers may become frustrated with that flexibility. Since there is client buy-in at each sprint, the changing targets are not a bad thing. The most important functionality will be in place where it is prioritized through the process. The client is driving the process, so IT leadership need to adjust their thinking to embrace the methodology that is enhancing their success.

5. **Agile is not good for very large applications.** If you have thirty developers across the globe working on pieces

of the same application, the application needs to be well designed in advance to portion out the pieces and how they interface with one another. Daily scrums with thirty people or across many time zones are also not practical. However, using rapid application development tools (RAD), you can still deploy prototypes earlier for testing purposes using the waterfall methodology and get feedback before the beta testing process. It's not as flexible as Agile, but it helps mitigate the gaps in client participation inherent in the waterfall methodology.

6. **Agile can still work for very large efforts.** While individual Agile projects don't scale upwards well, a program effort with a large number of smaller Agile projects can still work. In fact, efforts such as the Scaled Agile Framework (SAFe) use what they call Agile release trains (ART) for program management of multiple Agile projects. There is another level above the programs for managing the enterprise portfolio. While SAFe is one of the better organized attempts at scaling Agile, it's not without its detractors.

Agile methodology may be applied to non-software-development projects, but its application not well defined and often misapplied. For example, most technology infrastructure projects are not usable by clients at all until they're complete; the waterfall method still works best for them. Sure, you can use scrums for daily team communications with any type of project using any methodology, but that alone doesn't make the project Agile.

Agile and Lean Terminology
If you are investigating or using Agile methods, the Lean methodology first used by Toyota in manufacturing is often intermixed. If you want to use either or both, you're in for learning many new words and also new word meanings for old words (many more than scrum, sprint, and train). I've tried to keep the new vocabulary to a minimum here with the bare basics to avoid making this section a glossary of new terms. Frankly,

they probably went overboard a bit on repurposing words like story, epic, and velocity. Insisting on calling a ticket entered on a programming defect a "user story" seems unnecessarily confusing.

Lean also carries with it many Japanese words since it started with Toyota manufacturing. You may have heard of Kaizen (for continuous improvement) and Kanban (for just-in-time production). Various forms of waste are categorized by the "three M's" of Muda (work that does not add value), Mura (unevenness in workload), and Muri (overburden of existing resources). Somewhat ironically, **the traditional meaning of lean where you get by on as little as you can often leads to understaffing, which would be categorized as waste in Lean methodology** of Muri (overburden requiring staff working overtime) and likely also Mura (some staff taking more of the overtime burden than others).

While Lean principles were developed in the twentieth century, their application outside manufacturing has been more recent. Some people use "Lean Agile" methodology to represent the incorporation of Lean with Agile, though Agile may have partly grown out of trying to apply Lean to the software development lifecycle.

The main point to take away from Agile methods is the need for regular client interaction and involvement. **Agile requires a much larger time commitment from the clients in return for applications that more closely meet their needs.** Clients need to be testing the usable software developed in the last sprint and demoed at the sprint meeting while the developers are working on their goals for the current sprint. Waiting until you go into production with the software may uncover issues that should have been addressed much earlier and correcting the issues usually requires fewer resources the earlier they're detected.

Chapter 3: <u>Continuously Evaluate Technology</u>

This chapter is about selecting what technology to introduce when to meet business goals. Not every highly-hyped technology is right for your organization now. Conversely, you will miss out on some great opportunities if you don't integrate emerging technologies that are a good fit into your business processes. Knowing the difference is critical to your success.

Stay Informed

Read product announcements and reviews in popular technology news sites. Try to keep the sources in mind when evaluating information in articles; someone selling cloud services is going to make it sound great. Someone selling hardware and cloud services is going to give a more balanced view because they can make money either way, though of course their offering will be superior for the reasons they give. ☺

It's always good to keep tabs on whom the players in a particular market in which you buy products are. You don't need to do resource-intensive research until a few months before your procurement process begins. If you're sending out requests for proposals (RFP), you want to make sure that all the main vendors are included in addition to any your procurement services department may add.

Evaluation Criteria

Whether you're evaluating hardware, software, or services, there are a few bases to cover to make sure you have the information you need to make the best decision for your business.

Security

Security as an afterthought invariably results in poor security. This has been proven time and time again. So, when evaluating a new product or service, start with whether it will make your data more or less secure. If the answer is more, then that's great! If less, be thinking about what steps might be taken to eliminate or at least mitigate the increased risk. If the risk isn't acceptable, then neither is the product or service.

Avoid Vendor Lock-in

Think ahead. For any product or service you implement, at some later point you'll need to replace it or deprecate it. How easy will it be to replace with a different vendor's product? If you're locked in to a product, you're at the mercy of the company that provides it for continuing support at whatever price they believe the market will bear. Which competing products offer a more vendor agnostic platform?

For example, be wary of a service that has lots of helpful tools to import your data, but nothing to help export it in a usable format. Also, watch out for hardware that only works with specific software.

Price

This one seems almost too obvious to mention, but pricing can be quite obtuse. Are you buying a perpetual license where you can use whatever it is as long as you like, or is it more like a lease where you must pay an annual fee to keep it in service? If there is an annual fee for software maintenance, does it start the first year, after the first year, or sometime thereafter? How much does it cost? Does the annual fee cover software upgrades (some just cover bug fixes) or are they an additional cost? If you prepay for support/maintenance at the time of purchase, what kind of discount can you get?

If you expect the useful life of a product to be five years, then you should calculate the total costs for the five years when comparing with other products that include initial costs, maintenance, support, upgrades, etc. You might have to use current pricing extrapolated to future years, but something is better than nothing. I'm not including expansion in this, but if you expect to expand it (storage, for example), you should also compare those separately.

One extra caution on software pricing: make sure that you understand the licensing terms in relation to where you run the software. Some licenses are favorable when virtualized (like using Microsoft Server Data Center CPU licenses to run any number of instances in a virtualized environment) while others seem downright hostile to virtualization (wanting you to license every CPU core in the cluster when you only want to run on one virtual machine). This goes double for moving to the cloud; you may find that your site licenses don't apply since they're not running at your site. You may not qualify for a special discount you're used to getting if not running on hardware you own (this is not unusual for academic or non-profit license terms). You really have to remember this twice: when purchasing the software for one environment and when you're thinking of migrating it to a different environment.

Performance
Performance is always going to be relative to some other product or standard. Issues include what kind of performance is acceptable during peak load versus the usual load have to be solidified. For most services, peak load is also the most critical time for the service. For example, a retail application that works fine ten months out of the year but can't handle the Christmas holiday rush would be considered a failure because almost half of the year's revenues are dependent on those two months. Good performance 92% of the time may sound great (ten months plus nights twelve months of the year), but when 8% of the time counts for up to 75% of the annual profits, that failure could bankrupt a company dependent on retail sales.[5]

Another metric to consider is the Price/Performance ratio. So, if something is twice the price but gives four times the performance, it has a favorable ratio. In reality, it's more about what performance you need... if you need as fast as you can afford, then the price/performance ratio is going to be significant to you. If the slowest product offering is sufficient for your needs during peak usage, then you're going to focus more on features and straight pricing.

Features and Reliability

Feature sets are very dependent on what type of hardware, software, or service you're evaluating. One of the ways to develop a feature set you want to review is to gather information for several products and see what features they offer. Which ones are the most important to your organization? Develop a list of each feature. **Prioritize the feature list without a particular product in mind and don't forget to include requirements that you assume all products will provide.** Then, rank each product for how well it supports each feature. If a product offers excellent support for your high-priority features, it's probably a good match for your needs. Often, though, there's a mix of how well a product implements features of various priorities, and you have to use other factors to help in the decision-making process.

Stating "unstated" assumptions first thing is helpful and you may add appropriate ones to your features list. Here are two reasons:

1. You can challenge an assumption once it's stated. Is this really a requirement?
2. Others reviewing your assessment of products may not have the background to know, "of course it has to do that".

One oft-overlooked feature of products is how quickly they support new versions of related products. For example, with backup software, how long after a new version of an operating system or database is released before it's supported by the product? If it's more months than you can count on one hand, how might that impact your upgrade plans? I remember one product had a definite support problem, not supporting new versions of operating systems or databases for almost two years! That alone took it out of the running as a product we wanted to consider.

I include reliability with features because it is often what recovery or redundancy features a product has that influences its reliability. How critical the product is to your service and how critical the service is to your organization will determine how much weight you want to place on reliability when evaluating it.

Resources to Manage
I can't emphasize the importance of this enough! When you are trying to make the most of the resources you have, you have to take in to account what the management overhead is for the product or service. If the best product on the market takes a team of five to manage and you have half of one person's time available for it, it's not a good fit for you. For a typical mid-sized business, some products won't scale up to your size (ones intended for small businesses) and some won't scale down (ones intended for large enterprises). **If vendors supply you with a current list of some of their clients, see how many are your size.** If there are a few, see if you can contact them to talk about their implementation and what resources they're using to support it.

I've seen a lot of money wasted by not accounting for the human resources required to manage products and services. There are several product areas that have a huge diversity of support requirements between products. I have also seen that the better designed products are typically easier to manage, so you'll likely profit from both less time to manage and a more stable product offering.

Contingency Planning
Any new product or service needs to have your current contingency planning process applied to it. Where does it fit in terms of business impact analysis (BIA)? What steps may be needed to ensure business continuity (BC) and disaster recovery (DR)? You don't want to implement something that you can't

support all the way along your contingency planning process. Giving it some thought before you purchase can save you time and money later because you can design this in from the beginning. If you want a closer look at contingency planning, see another book I wrote called *Planning for Disaster: A Business Survival Guide*, available from the same sources where this book is sold.

Example Evaluation: Storage Area Network (SAN) Hardware

 Warning!
Geek
Speak

2016 Update Note: Dropping prices on solid-state disks (SSD) are changing the storage picture dramatically. There are some forecasts that their cost per gigabyte will drop below traditional disks sometime in 2017. New memory types are appearing in them as well. In addition, new filesystems and interfaces like non-volatile memory express (NVMe) are being proposed to take advantage of their potential speed instead of just pretending to be a really fast spinning disk. **If this trend indeed continues, traditional spinning hard disks will likely become a storage medium of the past like floppy disks.**

Storage tiers would also likely pass away since all storage would be SSD; the only way tiering will stay around is if the properties of various SSDs make it advantageous to use multiple types in storage arrays.

Google has also been publishing their experiences with all types of disks; one surprising finding is that the age of SSDs is more of a determining factor in failure rates than how many times they have been written to in the same locations (this was thought to be the determining factor in SSD lifetime). SSDs evidently routinely fail well before they reach their advertised write limits.

I'm leaving the following example largely unchanged for two reasons:

1. The areas to consider for evaluation haven't changed, just the types of solutions you'd be considering.
2. It's an example of how just a couple of years can affect the options you consider, underscoring the need to stay informed. I've seen folks purchase solutions that would have been considered very good three to ten years before but are currently both outdated and add unnecessarily complexity.

So, without further ado, here is the example evaluation from 2014:

First, we bring some knowledge of various drive types. The common ones are solid state disks (SSD) that are really NAND memory and not disks at all, serial-attached SCSI (SAS) hard disk drives (HDD), and drives that are either SATA or SAS with higher capacity but slower. The easiest way to tell between a "regular" SAS drive and one that shares the SATA design with a SAS interface is the rotational speed: performance SAS drives will spin at 15K or 10K RPM while their slower cousins will spin at 7,200 or 5,400 RPM. The faster they spin, the lower the rotational latency of the disk and the faster they can read data once it's under the head.

SSDs are very fast and expensive (the faster and longer lifetime single-layer cell (SLC) SSDs ran about $30/GB in 2014). SAS HDDs are much less expensive (a bit over $1/GB) and perform well for most enterprise applications. SATA/SAS HDDs are about a third of the cost per gigabyte of their SAS cousins, but are slower and not meant to be hammered on 24x7 (without a high failure rate). They are good for storing data that isn't accessed as often. Even as I'm writing this book in 2014, prices for some SSDs are plummeting towards the $2/GB mark, making an all-flash array affordable for midsize businesses for the first time. This is the year you'll see more and more vendors offering all-flash arrays.

All three types of drives are common in modern SAN implementations. The last several years, automatic storage tiering has become a great addition to SAN features. This means you buy a mix of the drive types and let the storage controller move data around based on how frequently it's accessed. Your "hottest" data lives on the fast, expensive storage and data that got written and only gets accessed during backup lives out on the slow, cheap storage. [If you read the 2016 update at the beginning of this section, you know that tiering is likely on its way out.] I'll write more about this when we get to the features section.

Security – this will likely be very similar for SAN solutions as long as you're on the same network infrastructure. Comparing multiple fibre channel (FC) solutions is relatively simple. If you throw iSCSI into the mix, that runs over Ethernet switches instead of FC switches (or directors). With FC, you're likely only attaching SAN servers and storage and there's no remote access. With Ethernet, you have to go back to making sure you're using a common denominator. For one thing, successful iSCSI implementations require non-blocking high-end routers and switches. If you're going to create a separate storage network with high-end gear for your SAN, you've brought it back into similarity with your fibre channel network. If you're going to use the same backbone architecture for your network and storage traffic, you have to be more careful about your setup and factor that into your security considerations. Converged network interfaces fall between the two, as there is one interface at the server side for both network and storage that later is broken out to FC and Ethernet.

Avoid Vendor Lock-in – this is one of those cases where everything is relative. You're likely going to have to buy drives with particular firmware on them for the SAN appliance you choose. However, it should not tie you into a particular vendor's interface cards on servers or particular FC switches. However, SANs are complex when it comes to compatibility, with, from the server to the storage, the following version dependencies:

1. firmware on the server interface card
2. operating system device driver for the above
3. firmware on your SAN switches or directors
4. firmware on your SAN controller
5. firmware on your SAN disks

Minimum versions of each will likely be required and upgrades have to take all of them into consideration (making planning SAN upgrades a non-trivial headache), but making sure all these have been considered before a new purchase is important. You have to double-check that the new SAN controllers and disks will fit into your existing network or know what other upgrades will be required for it to work.

Price – this one is again easiest to compare the more similar the storage options you are considering. Some companies bundle a lot of functionality into the base price, and some will cause you to roll your eyes at them with "options" for what we consider basic functionality ("Oh, you want to be able to see how much space is not allocated? We have a reporting option…"). Aside from the licensing mire, you also want to work on price/performance ratios for SAN storage because that's really a major significant difference.

Performance – this is a major differentiator in storage options. I/O bandwidth and latency are a major factor in virtualized environments and you want to make sure your SAN isn't slowing it down. This is where you need to determine the right mix of SSDs, SAS, and near-line SAS or SATA disks for the performance you need. If twenty percent of your data is accessed eighty percent of the time, then the other eighty percent of your data that's only accessed twenty percent of the time doesn't need to be taking up expensive storage all of the time. Auto-tiering features that move data between performance tiers can also reduce the amount of faster storage you need. [2016 update: All-SSD arrays may eliminate tiering unless the properties and costs of future types of SSDs lead to enough differentiation to warrant using tiered storage.]

Features and Reliability – this one needs a comparison chart for all the products you're evaluating. You need to ask a lot of questions of sales support engineers. Questions like "what happens to my data when I add another disk to the set" need good answers. The best solutions have storage virtualization that spreads data out evenly between disks of the same type. If this process is not automatically done, it can lead to "hot spots" for your I/O where all your most recent data is plopped on the last disk you added. Spindle count is also important for logical disks as, up to a point, the more parallel I/Os that can be done to read your data in, the better your performance. So, storage virtualization features are important for performance. We've already discussed auto-tiering benefits for performance. It is a more recent addition (introduced in storage products in the last five years), but with the gaining popularity of SSDs, it's even more important (unless you can afford and justify an all-SSD array for everything). [See 2016 update; all-SSD arrays are much more likely.]

Reliability may be determined by historical data, if it exists, but redundancy is one measure you can use. How many controllers can fail? How many drives in a disk group? Without virtualization, with near-line SAS or SATA drives, a minimum of two-disk redundancy per set is usually needed (using RAID6 or its equivalent) or mirroring. With production SAS or SDDs, single disk (using RAID5 or its equivalent) or mirroring is more common. Within virtualized storage groups, there is usually a "vRAID" equivalent as well. Some arrays always mirror data and you can choose how many mirror instances there are for specific data. Most solutions also try to allow for the failure of an entire shelf; data needs to be spread across shelves, not just drives for redundancy.

Resources to Manage – this can vary widely and should not be overlooked. If the SAN array still uses technology from the 1980's and 1990's, you might have to use a spreadsheet to keep up with what disks are being used in what RAID set for what logical disk. Unfortunately, there are still several solutions on the market that haven't embraced storage virtualization. Hopefully, they at least have spent some of the last decade developing a nice graphical interface that exposes such data so you won't have to resort to a spreadsheet to keep track. If your SAN supports automated storage virtualization and auto-tiering, on the other hand, you may have very little manual work or performance tuning to do, even when expanding the array.

Contingency Planning – before purchase time is the best time for planning this. If you need a hot site running somewhere, you might be in the market for two SAN arrays that synchronize between themselves. Perhaps you have an array that can synch with the new one already? There are lots of options to consider for replication. If you have a second location nearby, you can use synchronous replication and keep both arrays at the same recovery point. If it's farther away (safer from a disaster recovery standpoint), you might need to use asynchronous replication to keep them not quite so tightly synchronized. On the other hand, perhaps off-site tape backups will fit the bill for your recovery point and recovery time objectives and you don't care how well the array supports replication. It all depends on the needs raised by your business impact analysis, business continuity, and disaster recovery planning.

I hope this SAN example has proved helpful. I did not go into much detail on particulars with specific products because that data is outdated within months.

 Returning You
to Non-Geek
Speak ☺

Chapter 4: <u>Compare Products and Services</u>

In elementary school math class, we learned that we had to have a common denominator to compare or add fractions. Comparing products and services is much the same; you have to try and evaluate them on a common basis. You can't get anywhere comparing apples and oranges unless you first convert them to a common fruit base for evaluation.

The last section was all about evaluation criteria. Once you have an objective way to compare products, each of those criteria must be evaluated. One of the most important rules here is not to make assumptions or take anything not explicitly stated for granted.

One "common denominator" area of caution is migrating capital expenditures to operational expenditures for technology. When comparing in-house with outsourced options, there is often this trade. Many businesses seem to prefer this for accounting purposes. However, consider the scenario of having a poor year and undergoing budget cuts. If you have equipment that you can defer replacement on or software that you can delay upgrading for another year, you can keep running on it for just the cost of maintenance. If you're paying for cloud resources, reductions are going to be much harder to manage. You may have to reduce the number of servers where it will poorly impact performance or eliminate a service altogether. Your provider isn't going to leave your server or service running if you can't pay for it.

Example Comparison: Servers in the Datacenter versus Servers in the Cloud

First, let's work on stating our unstated assumptions:

1. We're only evaluating standard size servers; this keeps things simple for both scenarios.
2. The servers need storage, so we need to account for that. The storage will need to be near the servers because of latency requirements.
3. The storage needs to be backed up so that deleted files can be restored according to our internal service-level-agreement for file restores.
4. We're going to assume the applications on the servers don't depend on low-latency access to a database in our datacenter.

Now, let's take each of the criteria from the previous section and see how things stack up.

Security

Everyone is so excited about the feature possibilities of cloud computing that the security concerns are usually glossed over. However, going to an off-site location with the equipment owned and managed by a vendor involves significant increased risks.

The first rule of computer security is physical access. Anyone that can physically access a system can compromise it. With your own datacenter, you keep the door locked so that only your authorized employees have access. Vendors are usually escorted by employees when in the datacenter. Using a cloud vendor, not only do you not control who can access the equipment your server is running on, you don't even have such access. If your vendor's employees or their subcontractors want to get everything you have there, they can.

A mitigating factor for this lack of control over your server and data off-site is using encryption. There are basically three scenarios here, from least to most secure:

1. All data is encrypted at the hardware level but is presented unencrypted to your guest server. This keeps data from being read in the event that the actual hardware falls into

someone else's hands, whether by swapping out disks and them being resold by the maintenance vendor as refurbished drives with the data still on them [yes, this happens], or in the event the hardware is sold or traded in. Anyone with access to the server can easily read the data because it requires no changes at the server level.

2. All "at rest" data at the guest server level is encrypted. This means that your database is encrypted, but the key is also present to decrypt it for reading and writing. Your data is unencrypted in the server memory and a third party, with the key that's there, could also decrypt it with that key.

3. All data sent to the server is encrypted. The decryption key is never sent into the cloud. While this is the most secure, it's really only practically useful for long-term data archival. There has been some work on encryption that would enable manipulation of encrypted data, but none of it has made it to the product phase as yet. Craig Gentry with IBM has proposed something called "fully homomorphic encryption" that would add an "evaluate" function to the public-key functions "encrypt", "decrypt", and "keygen" commonly in use today. If this comes to fruition, then we will be able to manipulate data without decrypting it and finally be approaching security near that of on-site.

One problem with any encryption that uses algorithms where the difficulty in decrypting them depends on factoring large prime numbers is that they are vulnerable to a brute-force attack. Some people think that quantum computers will make such attacks trivial in the future, meaning that any encrypted data today might easily be read at some point in the future. On a less futuristic note, sometimes weaknesses in the algorithms expose short-cuts to decrypting the data that make the resources needed to do it fall drastically short of what was intended. The most secure data is still the data that you can't access in any form, encrypted or not.

After physical security, securing the operating system level is next. With virtualized environments, that means both the host operating system running on the hardware and the guest operating systems running on the virtual servers. With cloud operations, the host-level security depends on who's managing the cloud. The guest level will likely be a shared responsibility.

Application security is the next layer up. Depending on the type of cloud operations, this may be either your or a shared responsibility. Application security varies greatly by architecture, so this is an area you'll have to investigate for each application.

After all the layers associated with the server comes access to it: network security. Restricting the ability to reach the server to the minimum set of networks and ports reduces the attack surface. You may have limited ability to control what servers are on the same network as your own in the cloud. Virtual local area networks (VLAN), virtual firewalls, and virtual private networks (VPN) are all factors that can come into play to keep your network secure and ones that you have either no or shared control of in a public cloud environment. Compliance with certain security standards like the payment card industry (PCI) takes a lot of very careful planning in the cloud.

It doesn't take a genius to see that public cloud offerings have drawbacks in a number of security areas. **What is really important, though, is your risk assessment**. Want to share public information in the cloud? All you really care about then is maintaining the integrity of the data (so someone else can't change the information you're sharing). Having any number of people able to read it is not an issue. The security found in today's cloud offerings is typically sufficient.

Want to put confidential or sensitive information in the cloud? Your organization will have to decide whether the additional risks are acceptable. There are definitely different levels of sensitivity; personally identifiable information such as employee names and addresses aren't as sensitive as their social security numbers.

Information being used in an active lawsuit is usually more sensitive still. Just don't be lulled by a false sense of security by the number of other folks doing it; if your data is compromised, people won't be looking at how many others also put their data at risk; they will justifiably be blaming you.

Another issue with sensitive information in the cloud is what your vendor might legally share with others without your knowledge. If they're served with a search warrant, your company's data may be gone before your own legal department even has a chance to react. If it's a sealed warrant, you may never know that your data was shared. At least when it's on-site and controlled by your employees, you know what goes out when. Subpoenas are another area of concern. Typically, vendors require them to be served to the customer rather than complying with them themselves. But, if your cloud vendor is smaller and doesn't have their own legal team to fight these, they may end up surrendering your data because they can't afford the legal costs to say they shouldn't.

One caution about your risk assessment: it needs to be ongoing. It's very easy to start using cloud services without sensitive data and then keep adding applications and data that is more sensitive without realizing the security tradeoffs you were willing to accept with the less sensitive data.

Avoid Vendor Lock-in

This applies equally on-site or cloud-based. On-site, this translates to using as much commodity hardware as you can that's easily replaced by another vendor's. Depending on the granularity you desire for this, blade systems may or may not be a good fit. In the cloud, this means choosing clouds with as many open standards as possible for both platforms and interfaces. Ideally, cloud management that you can run internally as well as in a public cloud is going to have the least vendor lock-in for you. If you can migrate your virtual servers to a vendor cloud and back to your internal cloud with just the click of a button, you have done very well.

Price

This is where it starts getting tricky comparing on-site with off-site services. You need to compare the total cost of ownership (TCO) with each option. For on-site, this means apportioning a fraction of the datacenter costs for a server including floor space, racks, cabling, power, monitoring, and operations staff. You also need to do the same for the storage required for those servers. Network costs should also be included; perhaps you already have a per-port cost estimate that covers the switches, routers, and firewalls? Of course, the actual cost for the server hardware goes into the TCO, too. ☺ For off-site, the overhead includes the personnel time spent negotiating and reviewing contracts and service level agreements. It also includes whatever interfaces may need to be purchased or developed for integration with existing services. Also, apportion out a part of your Internet router and bandwidth costs based on what percentage of the traffic will be added by this new server on average. Add that to the pricing you get from your cloud vendor to make TCO there.

That covers the hardware aspect. Software pricing must also be considered, especially if you can't use existing site licenses or discounts when you move to the cloud and are running on someone else's hardware. If you're trying to do a general on-site versus off-site server comparison, this could be difficult trying to weigh the differences in all possible software you might run locally or in the cloud. If you are doing this with a specific project in mind, you can use actual costs of all the software involved, though you may need to meet with your software vendors to work out licensing details and how they pertain to the cloud.

Performance

In theory, this should be an easy comparison. You can compare the number of cores and CPU speeds, amount of memory, and disk storage for various configurations. That'd be it if the vendor site was next door. Unfortunately, network latency and bandwidth issues make the off-site cloud an entirely different prospect. Let's assume that we're using a technology that doesn't have problems with higher latency like web services. If it's just serving up web pages with text and graphics, your performance degradation should not be that noticeable. If you're running a web-based file server, though, your on-site downloads are going to run at a fraction of the speed they would if the servers were on-site.

The take-away here is that you have to evaluate each usage of an on-site versus cloud server. In many cases the performance will be completely acceptable almost all of the time. I use "almost" because there are a number of additional factors in getting the service from off-site. For example, if any of the Internet backbone carriers between your site and your cloud vendor's site experience intermittent bandwidth or routing issues, they will show up in your service as well. You may have performance problems that are neither your or your cloud vendor's responsibility nor under either of your control.

This is another case of price/performance consideration, though you're not necessarily working with specific numbers here. You have to decide if the standard performance of the cloud solution is acceptable and what price advantage is sufficient to accept lower performance. Even in the web-based file server example, if files aren't downloaded frequently or it is customer-facing so that diverse locations are the norm, the much slower performance would still be completely acceptable.

Features and Reliability
This is an area that takes a lot of research to evaluate, especially if you're comparing your one single datacenter to several cloud offerings. Each one of the cloud offerings will be different in what it offers, and avoiding assumptions about features and reliability is critical to your comparison.

For feature comparisons, you should make a chart of all the features you want and all the features that any of your cloud vendors provide. Fill it in for both your on-site options (maybe two columns if you want to compare your current virtualized environment with expanding it into an internal cloud) and each of your cloud options. Once you have this common-denominator chart, prioritize each of them. If you want to be analytical about it, assign a weight to each category and give each option an overall score. You can then weigh those scores in with other factors such as price to make your decision.

Some features tend to cancel each other out. For example, one feature folks like to tout is the predictability of costs in the cloud. On the other hand, the ability to automatically scale your servers for the demand (cloud bursting) is another feature that can be very useful, but also means that your budget for your cloud servers can also have the same bursts. Perhaps if you can reliably predict these spikes in demand, you can still budget for them, but one of the best features for going with a vendor cloud is not having to devote the time and resources to carefully plan capacity as you would for an internal cloud or your virtualized environment.

Make sure you include comparing the mechanisms for distributing your software on newly provisioned servers and how much of the common tasks you handle versus those of your cloud provider. As long as you use their tools, many of them will handle quite a bit of this for you. If you're comparing to an internal cloud in your datacenter, don't forget to make the same comparisons – you might not have your cloud as automated as theirs.

You should include security measures as a feature in your chart, though we've talked about it separately. If you're evaluating public information services for the cloud, your measure is going to be how they safeguard your data from being manipulated rather than securing it from being read by people who are not authorized. As I've stated elsewhere, using the cloud for data that's not sensitive has little downside and the ability to burst it for huge spikes in demand is one feature that is expensive to provide in a private or internal cloud but incurs no overhead costs in the public cloud.

If you've done your risk assessment and decided that the risks of a public cloud are acceptable for some sensitive data, you'll want to have more specific security comparisons. You need rows for criteria like enforcing encryption and at what points, what other servers may share your network, what are the firewalls like and are servers other than yours behind the same one, are any compliance issues met, etc. Ideally, you'd want to include all this information in a risk re-evaluation before you proceed.

Resources to Manage

This is another tricky area. Many people naïvely think that cloud options won't require much in terms of local resources to support since the hardware portion is out of the picture. How much of your staff's existing time is really spent on "racking and stacking" hardware, though? If you're managing everything from the operating system on up, you're not facing a significant savings in resources in terms of server management. In addition, the management interfaces into your cloud provider may prove to be more cumbersome at times.

The big savings here is in the level of automation for the initial server provisioning. Most cloud providers will have things highly automated. If you're virtualized but not highly automated on-site, you could save considerable time by choosing the cloud option. You might consider the differences in implementing an internal cloud versus off-site cloud.

A part of the server provisioning savings in the cloud is the physical capacity for the virtual servers. If you are comparing a major cloud provider to yourself, things like provisioning an extra hundred servers are no sweat in the cloud, but you might need to purchase physical hardware if you don't have that spare capacity when doing it on-site.

Contingency Planning

If your organization has done contingency planning, you're used to doing business impact analyses (BIA), business continuity (BC), and disaster recovery (DR) plans. You should use the same depth of planning for cloud options. Don't assume your cloud vendor has this covered.

The big cloud players usually make the news with their outages, so I don't have to tell you that they experience hours or days at a time of unexpected downtime despite all the redundancy they may have. In some cases, you can pay cloud vendors more to have your service available at multiple data centers in case just one is experiencing failures. I remember my favorite video streaming company having their service down on Christmas Eve because of problems at their cloud provider. So much for watching those Christmas specials in my queue! Because they also were pushing giving subscriptions as gifts, it was an especially bad time for them to be down. There are still times where their service doesn't work, but it's usually back the next day. When the outages are just a few hours, those often don't make the news.

Businesses that have made their own BC and DR plans for their cloud services have been very successful at keeping services available. Don't rely solely on your cloud vendor expecting they'll have the same sense of urgency to get the resources for your service running again. They are not going to be losing the revenue or experiencing the costs of downtime that you are. In most cases, their liability is limited to what you're paying them for the resources. Remember, if the service using the resources wasn't worth more to you than what you're paying them for the resources, you wouldn't be providing that service or paying them in the first place.

One company[6] was recently driven out of business by someone gaining access to their cloud provider console. After failing to extort money from the company, they proceeded to delete the company's customer's data and all the snapshots they had of it. In twelve short hours, the company announced they were forced to close. What little data they had salvaged, they helped their customers relocate. They had done test data recoveries, but it all depended on the one cloud. They thought they had everything covered, but malicious use of their cloud console wasn't something they'd considered. You should not rely on one cloud vendor for your contingency plans, but transferring data between clouds isn't something that's been standardized as yet. You'll likely have to develop your own mechanisms until the industry is more mature.

Chapter 5: <u>Emerging Disruptive Technologies</u>

Here are some technologies to keep evaluating because of both their impact and how rapidly they're disrupting the landscape not just of IT, but many vertical industries and even daily life for the average person. I write this section with some trepidation; I know it will "age quickly", and anyone reading this book years after it was written may find parts of it humorous in hindsight. Just think of it as a time capsule into the year 2014. ☺

2016 Update: I'm a bit surprised at how slowly some of these technologies have been adopted. Cloud computing has steadily been gaining traction about as expected. Big data seems to be moving ahead more slowly than cloud adoptions and the data retention concerns I raised seem to be one of the big factors. Another factor is that the analytics don't seem to be advancing as fast as demand for analyzing unstructured data. 3D printing advances have mainly been in the technology – implementations that apply it are still very much in their infancy. At some point, the technology advances will enable more implementations with less risk. I see this as a future major disruptor in the retail sector once people expect custom made products to be mass produced and affordable as such. Social and mobile targeting has proceeded the most rapidly of any of these disruptors. Virtual and augmented reality is just starting to see products ship to consumers this year after at least two years of hype about them; expect more in 2017. Last, but not least, technology for robots and connected devices has kept its advance. The FAA has implemented a registry for drone hobbyists. The "Internet of Things" (IoT) for connected devices continues to advance but is still plagued with too many incompatible standards and insufficient security.

Cloud Computing and Cloud Computing Architectures

First, what is the cloud? Network diagrams showing anything outside your network have a cloud to represent the network and hardware beyond your own, where you don't know what the network topology is. Your Internet service provider (ISP) is where "the cloud" begins for most organizations. For multi-site organizations, there is often a cloud between your sites to represent the carrier for your data lines. It's increasingly common to "piggyback" site-to-site connections on an encrypted virtual private network (VPN) over the public Internet, so the cloud is an appropriate representation. In summary, any goods and services you utilize that are beyond your network(s) are "in the cloud".

Cloud computing isn't new, but it is changing so rapidly that I include it as an emerging technology. Software-as-a-service (SaaS) has been around for decades under the name "hosted solutions". Hosted web services became prevalent soon after the web went main-stream and billboards started carrying web addresses. Infrastructure-as-a-service (IaaS) has also been around a while, though has grown rapidly with the wide-spread improvements in and acceptance of virtualized servers. Platform-as-a-service (PaaS), where you have OS, database, application environment (usually Java-based), and web server all with specific versions and guaranteed compatibility is the most complete of the server service base offerings that let you develop your own applications. Desktop-as-a-service (DaaS) is a fairly recent comer in cloud computing offerings, moving desktop virtualization into the cloud.

The modern **cloud computing architectures** are relatively new, however. They are invariably virtualized and far more automated than their predecessors. Applying this level of automation to your own servers on your own network is often called an "internal cloud", **redefining cloud computing to mean automation instead of location**. Such a redefinition of the term "cloud" is already gaining acceptance, even though it's confusing given its origins. People who use the phrase "internal cloud computing" really mean they are using cloud computing architectures and automation on a local network, not in the cloud. However, CIOs who want to be part of the latest and greatest hyped service (according to all the cloud providers and magazines that quote them) can say they're doing it now by implementing virtualization with some automation. ☺

Not to be confused with "internal cloud" (but it often is), "private cloud" is where your cloud vendor segregates your servers and storage from others. You don't share hardware with what they provide anyone else and shouldn't be on the same network (or subnet). An internal cloud is private unless you're selling cloud services to others, but private clouds can be anywhere. This is for people who have security concerns with a public cloud but are willing to let a vendor own and run everything in the cloud but give you more control over the resources. You might also contract a cloud vendor to run such services on your premises, in which case your private cloud is an outsourced on-site cloud.[7]

Just to try and keep things straight in this book, I've used cloud in its original sense of being off-site unless I qualify it with "internal" or "on-premises". You're not going to see such distinctions drawn in general publications, so keep in mind that the claims you read may apply to only on-site, only off-site, or both. You have to circle back around with some further analysis to determine what "cloud computing" claims are really claiming.

Software-as-a-service (SaaS) is perhaps the best cloud value because it includes everything needed to provide a service without having to worry about the layers underneath. SaaS offerings from the vendors who developed and sell the software are usually the safest. After all, if anyone knows what it should take to run it, they should. Of course, even they run into surprises with scalability when a customer is running a larger instance than they've run in their testing. One of the most well-known examples of SaaS is Salesforce.com with their sales, service, and marketing cloud offerings. Oracle is also hard at work fighting for market share against Salesforce. Microsoft has entered into SaaS in a big way with Office 365, offering e-mail, collaboration, word processing, spreadsheets, etc., giving Google Apps major competition. For the small business, offerings like these provide features that weren't feasible before because the staffing required to support the infrastructure and application servers. For large businesses, it requires much more analysis to decide whether to keep such services in-house or go with a cloud provider.

Web hosting services have been available from a variety of providers for many years. They provide a low cost of entry to web hosting; just about anyone can have a website. There are also several free options if you have a fairly simple static website and don't mind someone else advertising there around the edges of your pages. However, the newer cloud architecture services like Amazon Web Services (AWS) offer more in this area. For one thing, the automatic scaling based on demand for your web site provides what is known as "cloud bursting". This means that you can rapidly scale up your web infrastructure, such as right after a new product announcement that has a few hundred thousand folks all wanting to get the information at the same time. Once the "cloud burst" is over, it'll scale back down to more your usual load. You only pay for the extra resources while you're using them. This is attractive to businesses of all sizes.

Amazon Web Services offers a lot more than strictly web services. Despite the name, AWS offers several different infrastructure-as-a-service (IaaS) and platform-as-a-service (PaaS) products. They have competition from Google with their Compute Engine (IaaS) and App Engine (PaaS), Microsoft with their Azure cloud of Compute, Data Services, App Services, and Network product offerings, Rackspace (whose name reflects that they started as a hardware hosting company) with Public Cloud and Private Cloud offerings, and a host of others. This is currently a growing market, but I expect to see some of the providers (especially smaller ones with insufficient market differentiation) die off as the big guys keep pouring resources into this. The big-name hardware and software vendors are also elbowing their way into this market and I expect to see more and more from them. One advantage vendors have by their later entry is taking advantage of emerging open software for managing IaaS like OpenStack[8], and further up the stack with software like Puppet, Chef, Ansible, and Salt [9]. Hardware vendors can sell you servers and networking to run your own internal cloud or run it in their cloud with the same management portal and application programming interfaces. Software vendors can sell cloud services bundled with their own software where their licensing terms in other clouds make it cost prohibitive. I suspect that much of the current "cloud-hostile" licensing will eventually be changed to be more "cloud-friendly" if vendors want to maintain or reach a larger customer base in the future.

A recent new wrinkle in container virtualization is a product called Docker; it uses an application container rather than a virtual machine container. Red Hat and Ubuntu Linux distributions have already announced support for Docker and Google has some tools to help, too. It's too soon to tell whether this will turn existing clouds sideways as application virtualization could overtake server virtualization. The crystal ball for the cloud is still cloudy. ☺

The most important advice I can give about cloud computing is "Don't make assumptions!" This is especially true for services provided for other services. If you're looking at a cloud provider, you have to make sure the details are clearly spelled out. Just a few things to know:

1. What is their service level agreement (SLA) for time to restore files; how long ago can they have been deleted and how long will it take to get them back? Replication[10] is not

backup; files will be faithfully deleted on all replicas. Snapshots of data take a point-in-time view of the data. Snapshot retention and intervals are critical if you're using replication with snapshots to replace backups. Setting up snapshots may be up to you through a web interface; if so, you want automated options in addition to extra manual ones.

2. What are the limits on planned and unplanned down time? How long does a service have to be unavailable before it's considered an outage? Are all planned outages restricted to an outage window of time that you negotiated? What kind of advanced notice are you given for planned outages? What kind of remuneration will you receive to compensate you for unplanned outages? How do these apply to single server versus multiple server services?

3. What are the contingency plans for your servers/services? Do they provide multi-site active servers/services or failover? What are the recovery time (RTO: time to recover) and recovery point objectives (RPO: maximum time data is lost) for each service?

4. What countries will your data or services reside in? Are the current laws in those countries sufficient to protect your data from unreasonable disclosures? What are the risks?

5. How easy is it to get your data exported from that cloud and imported to another cloud or onsite? How usable is it in that form and how long would it take to bring up equivalent services? If the cloud provider goes out of business, are there third-party data broker agreements in place to provide this data to you? If their equipment is sold, what guarantee do you have that your data is safe from being read by whatever company purchases it?

6. How stable is the network between your sites and your cloud provider's sites? Are any of the Internet service providers between our sites allowing their routers to be

overwhelmed by bandwidth saturation? How slow might the services be during peak utilization?

You may be **very surprised** by some of the answers. Not everyone provides backup/restore. For those that use replication of storage, they may use it for their own purposes of recovering from hardware failures only. Are you compensated according to lost revenue or services when there are outages or is their liability limited to just what you paid for the service for the time it was down? Obviously, you aren't going to be purchasing a service that doesn't provide an equal or greater value to you than what it costs, but how much of that value can you recover if the service is unavailable? Don't assume their availability will be the same as what you are used to internally. If the last item on intervening networks is giving you trouble, there may be nothing you or your cloud provider can do to improve the situation without the additional cost of adding direct site-to-site networks between your sites and theirs.

I hope to see significant improvements in standardization and security that are needed before off-site cloud computing can really be considered a general use option. You definitely want to consider cloud computing, but the current hype about it exceeds its ability to deliver, especially off-site. **Today, most large enterprises would benefit from running internal clouds for general computing needs and only outsourcing to cloud providers for specific uses.** As with outsourcing, **small businesses can benefit the most from going to a cloud offering because they can obtain services that just wouldn't scale down to their size otherwise**. Small businesses often don't have the IT skills internally to adequately secure their infrastructure, so they may come out ahead in terms of information security (which is usually the biggest drawback for cloud computing at larger organizations). **Medium size businesses have to determine which is best suited for their needs because the trade-offs come closest to being similar for them.** Many will find starting up an internal cloud a challenge (taking steps beyond virtualization) but may find my advice for large enterprises also fits them best with the current state of computing in the cloud.

Big Data: Big Change for Analytics and Big Headaches for Storage

The promise of big data is that you save everything now and later you can mine it for useful information. Both structured (like traditional databases) and unstructured (like documents and presentations) data are thrown together. This goes far beyond data warehouses that merely aggregate structured data from multiple sources. Unlike traditional databases, you don't have to know up front how you plan to use the data and organize it accordingly.

Analytics and Business Intelligence

Analytics is basically the process of turning data into information. At a somewhat trivial level, charts and graphs within spreadsheet programs provide useful data visualization. With analytics, data is analyzed for patterns and anomalies. Analytics software can then use those patterns to predict future data (predictive analytics). Another term in common use for the analytic category of software is "business intelligence", though which one is the more specific term and which might include other technologies largely depends on who you're talking to. Just know that they're at least close relatives and I'll only be using the term "analytics" from now on.

Marrying analytics with big data requires new tools. Analytics software used to take well-structured data and turn it into understandable charts and graphs to aid in making decisions. With the addition of big data, analytics tools have to work much harder for two reasons:

1. The volume of data is often orders of magnitude larger. Getting timely results from queries takes some finesse.

2. The type of data can be almost anything digital: documents, images, spreadsheets, etc. Patterns can be more subtle across different types of media.

However, the opportunity for coming up with information that's more useful and covers a wider range of possibilities is intriguing. It takes a lot more "smarts" in the analytics software to handle the diversity and volume of data and turn it into something coherent and to the point. I look forward to seeing increasingly advanced analytics in the near future. **Better information provides the basis for better decisions.**

Storage

Saving everything means it has to be saved somewhere. The storage requirements for big data are significantly different from traditional databases, both from a hardware and software perspective. While traditional large databases are typically measured in gigabytes or even terabytes, "big data" often is measured in petabytes. If you're not familiar with the metric system prefixes, it takes a thousand gigabytes (GB) to equal one terabyte (TB), and one thousand terabytes to equal one petabyte (PB). When you get to storing that much data, traditional methods for accessing it and preserving it don't scale up well. Classic backups where you make a copy of the entire database at least once a week and incremental changes between just don't hold up well when it would take more than a day to get a backup. Different methods of data replication are typically used when working with large data volumes like this. Off-site copies are also typically done by replicating changed data to storage at remote sites.

Software

Cloud computing architectures are typically used for big data because of the scale required for storage and analysis. Apache software projects have a strong presence in the big data arena: Hadoop, Cassandra, and Hive are just a few of their most popular offerings. Google's MapReduce is another common software package used in conjunction with Hadoop. Using open source standards can help keep costs down, though many vendors offer their own flavors with their own support structures. Software in this area is rapidly evolving and there are many products. I expect to see an increase in the number of products before the inevitable shift in a few years' time to a handful for each type of big data cloud that come through as winners due to their rate of adoption and features.

Ironically, the cloud may turn out to be a mixed bag for big data; if your data is generated in different offsite clouds, pulling in to one "big data" repository might be quite the challenge. So while big data analytics and storage may thrive in a cloud environment, multiple offsite clouds will prove problematic for big data processes.

Another wrinkle for big data is one that your legal department probably won't like. It's very common to save everything past its normal data retention times in your big data repository. This means it also remains "discoverable" for legal actions and you might have to produce it under a subpoena. In fact, for unstructured data, it can be very hard to identify what retention policy should apply in the first place if you wanted to enforce your data retention standards. The possible rewards from big data analytics should outweigh the risks, but you might want to be choosy about putting the type of information that is commonly requested for legal actions into the repository without a way to expire it to adhere to your retention standards.

3D Printing: Mass Production Meets Custom-Made

3D printing has the potential to be the most disruptive technology in decades. It will likely turn a part of the manufacturing industry on its head as production keeps getting pushed closer and closer to the consumer. A computer-aided design (CAD) engineer can print all the prototypes he or she wants without requiring an expensive computer-aided manufacturing (CAM) assembly line for a wide range of products.

The following conjectures are one possible way this could unfold. The future in this area is pretty fuzzy because there are so many factors that come into play.

I don't expect the home 3D printer to be an immediate success. The speed, quality, and variety of material are limited while the pricing is still an inhibitor to major improvements in these areas. I think these factors will eventually be overcome, but it will take some time. Intellectual property rights for designs are also going to prove to be a sticky problem for some time to come.

If manufacturers want to take full advantage of this new technology, I predict industrial 3D printing factories will start popping up in major cities. Industrial 3D printers require less finishing work once the product has been printed and much of that can be done by robots right off the printer. They can also use a greater variety of material. Here's an example of how I see it working: You want a doll for your child. You order it and include pictures of your child with the order. The doll starts printing at a local 3D print factory and it looks like your child's twin on a smaller scale. Everything needed to complete your order is manufactured or warehoused locally. Depending on where the state of deliveries is at that point (maybe it'll get delivered to your door by a drone – maybe you'll go pick it up from a locker at your neighborhood drug store where it was delivered), you might have the toy the same day you ordered it, custom made. This is just one specific example of thousands of applications for this technology.

As you can see, this would also have a major impact on the package delivery industry. It would cause a shift to freight for raw materials to the factories instead of delivering finished goods from warehouses across the country. How much of a shift will be dependent on how popular this alternative method of manufacturing becomes. However, local deliveries should see increased emphasis whether it's getting it from the factory to your door or to a locker storage facility (likely paired with businesses already there) in your neighborhood. The latter would be a more likely scenario the farther away from the manufacturing point you get, with overnight delivery to lockers promised in more rural areas. Of course, as home 3D printing comes into its own, the shipping would shift back as small quantities of raw materials would be delivered to homes.

Another 3D printing enabler is getting custom-designed products to a market where it couldn't be afforded before. Prosthetic devices like artificial hands have made the news; improvements in design and adjustments in size for a growing child are just a re-print away.

The medical field is one of the major areas ripe for disruption. In addition to providing services in countries with fewer modern medical facilities, they are experimenting with 3D printing organ replacements. Sometime in the next decade, you might not have to wait for an organ donor for many transplant operations – a custom-fit organ would be printed before your surgery!

In conclusion, 3D printing will likely disrupt retail, manufacturing, and shipping industries. It will also change expectations on what kinds of products are available and how soon we can get them across all industries and home consumers. It has the potential to change the way we live, work, and play.

Social and Mobile Targeting

Your target audience for technology is expanding. Instead of customer relationship management (CRM), you're going to be targeting all *potential* customers with your services. Anyone who might use your business should be able to access all the potential information they could want in order to evaluate if they want to become a customer. Social networking makes spreading news by "word of mouth" include Facebook, Twitter, Instagram, Pinterest, and any number of other existing or future information-sharing apps. Talk about your services in other forums can exceed information they get directly from you and have a greater influence. You should be out there providing positive information about your services (but not "blatant advertising", just "sharing") in these forums. If your customer base can get help via tweets instead of having to call your helpdesk, you can score some points with the people using Twitter, for example.

Mobile and wearable computing also change the interface to your company information. Any customer website should have a mobile version that does more than just shrink or reorder frames because you know people will be going there on their phones and it needs to be usable. You never know what size screen you'll be seen on, from their TV to a smart watch. Accept the challenge to make the online experience a good one regardless. Wearable computing will also have a major impact on the next disruptive technology, virtual and augmented reality.

Virtual and Augmented Reality

Virtual reality is great for gaming, but meshing virtual with real is what augmented reality is all about. Most of the "real world" applications will be in augmented reality. Augmented reality depends on two things: a camera or optical scanner to take in reality, and a display to superimpose virtual images on reality. Most smart phones qualify for this, though the much-hyped glasses appearing on the market are less cumbersome. For those of you that watch American professional football, you're used to seeing lines that look like they're painted on the field to show the ten yards needed for a first down. You don't see the original image the camera is taking unless you're watching in the stadium; at home, it just looks like it's all real instead of virtually edited into the picture. Here are some other examples that exist today:

1. "Heads up" display (HUD) for fighter pilots showing information on their helmet displays.
2. Run a translation app and see signs in a foreign language translated to your language in the display, basically in real time.

3. Pick a piece of furniture from a virtual store and see how it would look in the room you are in, allowing you to move and rotate it as the app keeps the proper perspective... how would that coffee table look in my own living room?
4. Facial recognition software that puts names to faces for those of us with poor memories. ☺ This one has a lot of privacy implications for picking up additional information on people you don't know, too. "Hi, John Doe, how's your wife Jane doing today?"

Augmented reality has the potential to make video conferencing much more immersive by making it appear that people are actually occupying the space around you. While "presence robots" are a neat new thing, if everyone is wearing glasses that could superimpose images anywhere in your line of sight through them, it could blur the lines between who or what's really there and what's not.

I suspect the applications for augmented reality will just keep getting better and more prevalent across more industries. Microsoft hyped their augmented reality headset called "HoloLens" along with their Windows 10 announcement. It was very well received and I hope it makes it to mainstream usage. **There is great opportunity for innovation in this area with applications beyond any yet developed.** The jury is still out on whether most folks will be using their smart phones for it or allow it to be in their line of vision with HUD devices like glasses or helmets. From a usability standpoint, the latter gives a richer experience.

Robots and Connected Devices

Robots in science fiction have intrigued us for decades. Some of those robots have become a reality today, while we're still reaching for one that can make beds, dust, and answer the door. At least we have some that can vacuum the floor now. ☺

Most commercially-available robots have very specific tasks they can perform. A vacuum cleaner is one that I use, though I don't have it programmed to clean on a schedule because I have to pick up dining-room chairs and a few other pieces of furniture that tend to trap it and also keep it from doing as good a job. The manufacturers are always trying to improve on them and their artificial intelligence mapping out a room is quite interesting. Maybe they'll release a furniture-moving robot that can work in tandem with a vacuum robot to move smaller furniture out of the way and put it back when done. The vacuum might also get help when it gets stuck from its furniture-moving partner.

Another type of robot that makes the news a lot is the flying drone. The military uses them for reconnaissance and tactical warfare. Civilians use them to create aerial videos more than anything else. The laws governing drone use are still "up in the air", if you're forgive the pun. Civilian law enforcement use similar to military use understandably and justifiably makes people nervous. Private use also brings up all kind of privacy issues (yeah, now anyone can see over that fence around your back yard pool or look in second-story windows). The fact is, it's not just drone cameras but cameras just about everywhere that are invading our privacy. They even make Wi-Fi LED light bulbs with embedded cameras (a preview of connected device discussion). If you are out in a public place, you pretty much have to assume you could be on one or more cameras, but that is being extended to when we're on private property more and more.

The military is advancing robotics the fastest with their drive to replace human infantry. If you can make a machine that can go everywhere a soldier can and more and not risk a soldier's life doing it, that seems like a good goal. Of course, beyond reconnaissance and search and rescue missions is where things start to get on the scary side. When the robot infantry are armed and programmed to kill humans and destroy other robot infantry, we have to wonder where all this may end up. What happened to Isaac Asimov's famous Three Laws of Robotics to keep them from over-running mankind?

Robots are a growing area. I saw one article that had little robots that could work in tandem to move furniture around, raise or lower tables, carry items, etc., but depended on special grids that they could lock into be present on the furniture or walls. Tiny nanobots that can be injected into your body to perform all sorts of medical procedures are also coming closer to reality.

Connected devices are starting to make headway in places other than shows of smart homes. The media like to call this the "Internet of Everything" (IoE). Your thermostat, home appliances, lights, car, and anything else with electric switches or capable of being switched could all communicate to make a wonderfully efficient home experience. We will see a rapidly increasing number of these smart appliances very soon. In a few years, you may find it difficult to buy a "dumb" appliance or light switch. I expect the number of standards for connecting these smart appliances to dwindle so that more smart appliances can work with a wider range of other appliances.

While having your oven on the Internet and being able to tell it to preheat for your estimated arrival home (your smart phone or car would provide the estimate with your GPS and home address) might seem a really neat thing, having a hacker keep your oven on continuous cleaning cycles could take the fun right out of it. Likewise, hackers turning your thermostat to its maximum settings for heating or cooling could mean more than just expensive fuel bills. It could cause frozen pipes in winter or make the summer temps dangerously hot, especially for pets that might have been left home alone. If you can't manually override a hacked thermostat when you get home, you could also be driven from your house. Current home wireless networks just aren't secure enough to trust with your life.

Appendix 1:
Bandwidth versus Latency Blast from the Past

In the early 1990's, a common e-mail signature tag line was "Never underestimate the bandwidth of a station wagon full of magnetic tapes." To bring that up to 2014, we'll say "Never underestimate the bandwidth of a SUV full of LTO-6 tapes." The big SUVs can hold up to 130 cubic feet of cargo behind the first row of seats.[11] You can fit 120 LTO-6 tapes in one cubic foot. Each LTO-6 tape can hold 2.5TB of data (uncompressed). That means the SUV can hold 39,000TB (or 312,000Tb) of data. [T=tera, B=bytes, b=bits – capitalization counts when keeping your bits and bytes straight!] If the SUV maintains an average speed of 30 miles per hour, its bandwidth would be 2600Tb/sec. That's two million six hundred thousand gigabits per second going an average speed of 30mph.[12] For comparison, Internet backbone sites are currently utilizing hundreds, not millions, of gigabits/second bandwidth.

So, why aren't we seeing a bunch of SUV's with magnetic tapes running around carrying data? The obvious answer is because it's a very high latency solution. You've got the time to write the tapes, load them, unload them, and read them in at the target site. That's not to say data is never shipped. Most sites using storage replication technology first put up the replication partner locally where the bandwidth and latency are better. Once the new replication hardware is synchronized with the existing system, it's shut down and shipped. After it arrives at the destination and hooked up to the remote network, it works to catch up to the transactions it missed while being shipped. If it were shipped directly to the remote location and had to copy all the data from the original, it could take weeks to finish replicating (or, depending on the rate of data change and the bandwidth and latency between sites, months).

Appendix 2:
State of the Art and the Technology Lifecycle

The hype surrounding technology makes a lot of terminology meaningless. "State of the art" is where the art of technology is at its latest. For technologies still undergoing change, state of the art only lives in research labs. Only for very mature technologies where the art has not advanced in quite some time do people actually use "state of the art" technology, but by then so is everyone. Most marketing touting "state of the art" is total fluff; anytime I see it, the company using it loses credibility with me.

By the time a state of the art technology has been turned into a product, it's become "state of the practice" – the latest and greatest actually in use. This is where technologies are called "**leading edge**" and sometimes, only partially jokingly, "bleeding edge". The technology lifecycle is typically accepted to be a standard bell curve. On the leading edge, new features are the priority over stability. You can do things that most others can't yet, but you'll pay a price for it in terms of stability. Some leading edge technologies never make it into the mainstream, so there's also the risk of investing too many resources in something that proves to be transient. Everett Rogers, author of *Diffusion of Innovations,* calls people who use bleeding edge technology "**innovators**". Being an innovator is costly, but sometimes there are good business reasons to get out ahead of the market. If you're open to the risks of getting serial number 00000001 of a product, this is where you fit. ☺

Once a leading edge technology has been in use a while and stabilized somewhat, it's called an "**emerging technology**". People who wait to use a new technology until it has stabilized are called "**early adopters**". This is really the sweet spot of technology adoption – the technology has been proven enough to know it's going mainstream and you get to use it over the maximum of its lifetime. It's the most cost-effective time to adopt a technology. Whenever possible, you want your organization to be an early adopter of technologies that it uses.

Once a technology has been proven and is in general use, it's entered the mainstream. It's fine to adopt a technology at this point and is the most common option. If the technology isn't strategic for you, then you haven't lost much by missing the early adopter phase. In addition, market competition is usually stiffest here, so even though you won't have the technology as long to use, you may still come out ahead by getting it at a better price.

You don't want to be a late adopter on the trailing edge of the technology lifecycle curve. Try to avoid adopting mature technologies that only have a limited useful lifetime left. These are the folks who are jumping on the bandwagon when it's about to stop for good. Maybe you're migrating your applications to Unix when everyone else seems to be moving on to Linux. Even if a technology is superior, market acceptance of a different competitor can still spell the end. Consider the Betamax versus VHS battle in the home video industry. VHS won and Betamax faded into oblivion; years later VHS has joined it. Now, it seems that any physical media (including DVD and Blu-ray) is destined to become outdated as streaming is emerging as the new norm. The demise of physical media will have to be preceded by ubiquitous high-bandwidth Internet, though, so it's too early to abandon those formats now. ☺

About the Author

Harry Flowers has over thirty years of IT experience, about half of which has been in IT management. As an individual contributor, he has been a software developer, systems engineer, project manager, and infrastructure architect. He has managed all aspects of IT but is usually focused on infrastructure technologies.

Prior to this, Harry had been published as an author in technology certification study guides. Although he disappointed his fan base by not publishing again for many years, you are now reading the second edition of the work that marks his return to writing. After the first edition of this book, he also published *Planning for Disaster: A Business Survival Guide.* If you'd like to leave him comments about either book or even another topic you'd like to see treated similarly, feel free to e-mail him at hflowers@leaders4it.com.

End Notes

First, a short legal statement: **Any trademarks used in this book remain the property of their owners.**

---

[1] I will give one exception I've seen work to the technical leadership rule. If there are a lot of office politics, the CIO may spend their time providing political cover for what needs to be done. This only works if the CIO has a reliable CTO that he or she trusts. Strategic plans are made together and sales folk are told "You have to convince the CTO first."

[2] Peter Drucker, Ken Blanchard, Stephen Covey, and Peter Senge are just a few recommended authors of management books.

[3] Phishing is when hackers seek information from people that will help them compromise either their identity or computing resources. Spear phishing attacks target specific people or groups of people and the specifics in them, such as perhaps looking like they came from your C-level executives, make them more successful.

[4] It would cost millions of dollars to secure just one site. Faraday cages and non-algorithmic encryption would be just a start. Plus, if you go to that much trouble, you'll likely attract someone's attention for social attacks or infiltration to counter your security tech.

[5] Figures are from the *New Yorker:* "The Christmas shopping season can account for as much as forty per cent of a retail store's annual revenue and as much as three-quarters of its annual profit." http://www.newyorker.com/talk/financial/2007/12/24/071224ta_talk_surowiecki

[6] Code Spaces was forced out of business after touting their ability to protect customer data, but all their protection mechanisms depended on AWS. Once their console was compromised, all that went out the window. It could happen to anyone. http://arstechnica.com/security/2014/06/aws-console-breach-leads-to-demise-of-service-with-proven-backup-plan/

[7] In 2013, Amazon won a $600 million contract to build and manage a private cloud for the Central Intelligence Agency (CIA) at a CIA facility. This is an example of a private cloud run on-site that still isn't run by your own employees as an internal cloud would be. They can control the physical security of the site and have shared control of most other aspects. Since the federal government already makes extensive use of contractors with security clearances handling sensitive data, this doesn't represent a significant increase in risk from what they've already assumed.

[8] Rackspace (with NASA) started OpenStack and it's now an open source project with Apache licensing and many distributions. Companies providing distributions also typically sell support for their distribution; this is much the same for other open source cloud products mentioned.

[9] Cloud management software is changing rapidly; a comparison of these would be outdated before it went to print. Your best bet is to use web resources to research near the time you wish to implement.

[10] Replication is when an exact replica of your data is made. It is a more specific term than "copy", since you can have a copy of a file in a backup save set format. With data replication, the original data is replicated, then any changes to that are also replicated. Since only the changes are being transferred, it can utilize much lower bandwidth to maintain an exact copy than sending a whole database. Data de-duplication (not sending copies of data that's already there in a different location, just referencing it needs to be copied for this) and compression techniques can also provide huge savings in bandwidth. Replication may be synchronous (the original data change is not marked complete until the replica is updated) or asynchronous (where the update is allowed to complete after the data change). Synchronous replication is typically used when the replica is nearby because of latency issues.

[11] The vehicles referenced were a Ford Motor Company Expedition and General Motors Chevy Suburban.

[12] For a discussion on bits, bytes, and their metric multiples, see http://www.whatsabyte.com. I've used the 1,000 multiplier for converting GB to TB since we're talking tape storage rather than memory where 1,024 is commonly used, but both are common usage. Vendors tend to use the one that makes their statistics look better. ☺

www.ingramcontent.com/pod-product-compliance
Lightning Source LLC
LaVergne TN
LVHW052310060326
832902LV00021B/3797